You didn't build a great business by being timid

Owning a business means meeting new challenges every day.

But you've always taken on these obstacles with your instincts and your will to succeed.

A UBS Financial Advisor can help you move ahead with your business and your personal wealth.

Proceed with passion.

For some of life's questions, you are not alone. Together we can find an answer.

ubs.com/exitplanning

 UBS

EXIT RIGHT

EXIT RIGHT

HOW TO
SELL YOUR STARTUP,
MAXIMIZE YOUR RETURN,
& BUILD YOUR LEGACY

MERT ISERI & MARK ACHLER

LIONCREST
PUBLISHING

EXIT RIGHT
How to Sell Your Startup, Maximize Your Return, and Build Your Legacy

ISBN   978-1-5445-2601-0   *Hardcover*
         978-1-5445-2599-0   *Paperback*
         978-1-5445-2600-3   *Ebook*

*To Marcie Achler, the love of my life and
my life-long partner and inspiration.*

—MA

*To my late grandfathers, Mustak Hilmi Iseri and
Yasa Cetiner, who showed me that to be a great
leader, you need to be a great human being first.*

—MHI

*And to all entrepreneurs everywhere. To
the dreamers, the risk-takers, and those
with the passion and guts to change
the world. We're in your corner.*

CONTENTS

Foreword *by James Jack*   **xi**

Foreword *by Brad Feld*   **xv**

Introduction: The FAIR Framework   **xix**

PART 1: WORKING TOWARD A FAIR ACQUISITION PARTNER 1

1. How Fundraising Impacts the Exit   **5**
2. Building Trust Takes Time   **25**
3. When Is the Right Time to
    Begin the Actual Process of a Sale?   **43**
4. Who Are the Key Stakeholders?   **59**
5. What Does Corporate Development
    Want You to Know?   **87**

PART 2: NEGOTIATING THE RIGHT EXIT   101

6. Where Do Valuations Come From?   **105**
7. What Is a Term Sheet?   **121**

8. How To Maximize Value Throughout the Process   **161**

9. How To Keep Your Calm as the CEO   **179**

PART 3: CLOSING AND INTEGRATING FOR THE FUTURE   193

10. How To Get From a Signed Term Sheet to the Close   **197**

11. How Should the CEO Take Care of the Team?   **207**

12. What Are the Keys to a Successful Integration?   **225**

Conclusion: Most of the Journey Is Still Ahead   **239**

Acknowledgments   **247**

Disclaimer   **255**

Endnotes   **257**

FOREWORD

by James Jack
Head of Business Owners Segment Americas,
UBS Global Wealth Management, USA[1]

For business owners and entrepreneurs, a business exit is likely to be one of the most significant events of a lifetime. Beyond the financial outcome that impacts business owners and their families, a business exit will impact employees, investors, suppliers, and communities.

It's really difficult to start and grow a business. Every day is a new challenge, and it takes a special kind of persistence to be successful. Further, an entrepreneur's self-identification and legacy often become entwined with their company. A myriad of emotional aspects factor in, making the sale of a business even harder.

A lot is at stake when contemplating an exit. Yet too few business owners "begin with the end in mind." Most postpone planning for an exit until it appears closer on the horizon, if at all—which can be more problematic. In a survey UBS conducted, nearly half of the entrepreneurs who were expecting to exit said they had no formal plan in place. Thirty-seven percent said they had no structures in place to shield exit proceeds.[2]

People around the world are captivated by the idea of entrepreneurship and starting businesses that can help solve big challenges. It's a powerful notion that drives most growth entrepreneurs in their day-to-day efforts. So it's understandable why the "big picture" for them is on moving the business forward and problem-solving, not on what will happen—or can happen—when they turn over the keys one day.

As a world-leading global wealth manager,[3] UBS is home to Financial Advisor teams that are well versed in working closely with entrepreneurs and business owners. After all, successful business ownership continues to be one of the main drivers of wealth accumulation for families.

We spoke at length about the issues business owners face when we met with authors Mark Achler and Mert Iseri. In hearing their experiences as exited entrepreneurs and venture investors (along with many of the lessons they've gleaned from their extensive network over the years), so much of it rings true. UBS supports *Exit Right* because its authors and UBS share a common goal. We're all looking to help create better outcomes for entrepreneurs who want to make an impact and build a lasting legacy.

If you're part of the next wave of growth entrepreneurs, we hope you will take the lessons offered in this book to heart and work with a cross-functional team of financial, tax, and legal advisors to help put yourself in a better position when your venture concludes.[4] Start soon. Do it not to proceed with caution, but proceed with passion.

Reimagining the power of investing.
Connecting people for a better world.

That is our purpose at UBS and why we're excited to present Exit Right in support of you as an entrepreneur and the people and causes you care about.

FOREWORD

by Brad Feld

I wrote *Venture Deals: Be Smarter than Your Lawyer and Venture Capitalist* in 2011, with the hopes of demystifying what it takes to raise money for your startup. In the past decade, entrepreneurship has bloomed, with many more people starting companies every day. If *Venture Deals* is about how to fund the startup journey, Mark and Mert have written the book about how to conclude it.

Selling your company is hard work. It's the part of starting a company that nobody likes to talk about, yet every stakeholder wants to see it happen at some point. This book helps founders figure out how to make it happen the right way.

I've known Mark for many years as an investor with MATH Ventures. Mert is a CEO who has been through the trenches after a tumultuous exit with SwipeSense. They are both active within the Techstars community as all-star mentors who embody the "give first" spirit. The lessons they share in this book have been earned over many years through lots of challenging decisions.

I see mistakes in the sale of startups all the time. Sometimes founders think that their problems will go away if they can only sell them to someone else. The price may be less than what the company is truly worth, or buyers may overpay grossly without seeing the real return. Both situations are bad—bitter founders leave shortly if they believe their work isn't recognized, while unhappy buyers develop an aversion to future M&A, which hurts the ecosystem as a whole. While randomness and chance play a big role, founders and buyers can greatly improve the odds by playing the long game.

Trust is the most important element for exits to happen and for the integration to prove valuable down the road. This book takes the mystery out of the process by speaking to both sides while creating a framework that buyers and sellers can use to determine if this is the right partnership.

The FAIR framework (Fit, Alignment, Integration, and Rationale) describes the four elements that every founder and buyer should look for as they evaluate opportunities. It's imperative that founders realize that it is an active part of their job to ensure all the stakeholders are in lockstep via Exit Talks. Finally, the detailed discussion of the term sheet makes this book a worthwhile read for founders who are looking to level up their negotiation skills.

I encourage founders to dig deep into the concepts here, whether you are early and want to build an ecosystem of buyers or you are a later-stage founder gearing up for an exit. If you are having disagreements internally with your board or leadership about strategy or timing, make sure you are speaking the same language and share the same values on what you want to see happen in the future.

As for buyers, this is a great framework to build the case internally for why an acquisition makes sense. M&A executives can train their leadership or their product management teams to understand what makes deals work to avoid problems down the road.

Applying these lessons well can mean a difference of millions when the ink is dry on the closing documents and can change how you feel about what happens to your company down the road. Selling your startup should feel more like seeing someone you have been mentoring graduate from college, and you should be filled with pride and optimism for what is to come. This book will show you how to make that happen.

THE FAIR FRAMEWORK

I knew that after signing this piece of paper, my life was going to change forever.

The proudest moment of my professional journey was only a signature away. I was holding a term sheet that described the sale of our startup. After years of blood, sweat, and tears, we had successfully arrived at our exit.

Founders dream about their exits. We all know that you're supposed to focus on your customers and your team and not worry about the exit, but let's face it: we all do it. Although we sold our first companies decades apart, the feelings we experienced throughout the process were remarkably similar.

An exit means a lot of wonderful things aside from personal wealth. A successful exit means good things for virtually every stakeholder you care about in your startup: your team, your customers, your investors, and your family. All of those folks believed and invested in the dream: some with their money, some with their energy, some with both. It feels amazing to know that their belief in your dream will be rewarded.

When you sit down to sign the term sheet, an incredible feeling of accomplishment is shared by everyone involved. No matter the final price, everyone feels like they're receiving a golden ticket to their next big opportunity. For us, the final sale (Mark with the Whitewater Group in 1991 and Mert with SwipeSense in 2020) created a sense that we were finally part of the "initiated." We were in an elite group of people who can call themselves seasoned operators.

It's an overwhelming feeling—almost like a supercharged graduation from your dream school. The best part is that hopefully this isn't the end; it's just another beginning toward an even bigger dream. Startups are fragile—most of the time months away from shutting down their doors. The relief of knowing that your vision will continue for decades is similar to seeing land for the first time after months at sea (in a boat that almost sank five times). At least, that's what we imagine.

All of this is only a signature away.

But then, a second wave of feelings washes over you. Doubt creeps in as you start to consider a new set of individuals who now control your destiny. Once the term sheet is signed, there is no going back. This is the final destination. No matter what happens in terms of success, the cards are now fully in the hands of another entity.

Even worse is when feelings of doubt creep into the final sale price and you start to question if the buyers are paying what the company is truly worth. You get that nagging feeling of leaving money on the table. *What if we sold a year later? What if we sold to another company that could help our mission more? Are we agreeing to terms that will haunt us down the road? What the hell does indemnification even mean?*

A signed term sheet doesn't mean the deal is done—the stakes are high and the price to pay if things don't go as planned is hell. A botched exit means disgruntled investors, employees who lose focus, and, worst of all, customers who don't get the attention they deserve.

How, when, and if you sell your company is the biggest decision a founder gets to make other than deciding to start the company. It's bigger than the key hire, bigger than landing a signature customer, bigger than deciding to work with a particular investor. It's the ultimate decision of where you will call home, hopefully forever.

We wrote this book to maximize the first feelings and eliminate the second wave of feelings altogether.

Exit Right is the book we wish we had read before starting our companies. We have raised over $250 million in financing and have been personally involved in over $1 billion in exits as founders, executives, board members, and professional investors.

Before we start, it's important to get something out of the way: there's a reason not much has been written about how to sell your company. Today, it is taboo to even talk about the sale of your company with your board, let alone have long-term relationships with mergers and acquisitions (M&A) professionals. Influential investors like Paul Graham go to exceptional lengths to advise companies to never talk to corporate development. Most of the real wisdom in exits is buried underneath NDAs, and founders find themselves having to figure it out as they go through their first exit.

In a certain sense, Paul Graham is right: if you have built a rocket ship where sales are going through the roof, investors are banging down doors to write you checks, and top talent is fighting to secure a seat, you have nothing to worry about. In those circumstances, the exit does end up taking care of itself, given the competitive nature of larger companies needing to stay relevant. However, this isn't realistic for most companies.

We wrote this book to provide a practical reference on how to successfully exit right.

We want to emphasize this point: we are operators, not investment bankers. The information and advice in this book are the result of real lessons learned from real exits. We're giving you the knowledge that founders routinely pay 1–3 percent of their final price to understand.

We are not brokers. A broker can polish your business to make sure you are not leaving money on the table for things that are here today. They review your financials, double-check your legal agreements, support the negotiation by securing multiple bids, and more. In other words, a broker can push you toward the finish line, but you still have to run the marathon beforehand. This book isn't for the final mile; it's an overview of the strategic actions you need to take from start to finish.

Our personal experience—further shaped by the research for this book with over one hundred interviews with serial entrepreneurs, the biggest buyers from the Valley, and the best legal advice money can buy—tells us that the makings of a successful exit start years in advance. A banker can polish up what's already there, but we strongly believe that at best, their work results in an incremental improvement in the final price and the likelihood of closing. At worst, the banker does little, and their fees are simply a tax that gets deducted from the final price.

We want to be clear that there is no advice in this book that will suddenly make you or your company valuable overnight. Real value is created over years through trusted relationships and a strong rationale for long-term value. And although a successful exit means that the founders get rich, we think of

being rich as a side effect of the real win: creating a huge multiplier of impact by joining forces. Our objective is for you
to build the most valuable partnership you can through your
exit. Getting rich is delightful, but secondary.

This book is meant to be read in the early days of your
company. We believe selling a startup begins with the first
investment you accept. There are small, intentional steps that
founders need to take over the life of the company to execute
a successful sale. At the same time, remember that small missteps early on may set you on the wrong course and create long-
term damage. We want to ensure that doesn't happen to you.

To do that, we connected with serial operators with proven
track records to share their stories. They will share stories of
lessons they learned the hard way so that you can understand
what you're up against. We know that being a founder can be
overwhelmingly lonely throughout all of the challenges. We
want you to know that the great ones also struggled with
what you are going through and that you are not alone.

Our goal is for you to exit right and win both for the short
and long term. Maximize the price for your company while
finding the best long-term partner that positions you and
your company for a legacy you are proud of. Our hope is that
through this collected wisdom, you will improve your exit trajectory, and, in return, pay it forward to help other founders.
Please reach out to us if you find this book to be helpful with
your startup exit by emailing *community@exitrightbook.com*.

Let's now jump right into the framework that we will be visiting throughout the book. This is the overview of our findings on what makes a startup exit truly great.

THE FAIR FRAMEWORK

After countless interviews, we identified four common elements in that make acquisitions work. These are the elements that founders and acquirers should focus on to maximize the value of any transaction.

We call this the FAIR framework. It's what everybody wants, after all—a fair transaction. Founders want to be treated with respect and expect a return for their hard work. Acquirers want to avoid companies with skeletons in their closets or investing dollars in failed initiatives. In short, both sides want this to work out for the best: a scenario where one plus one equals one hundred.

FAIR stands for **fit**, **alignment**, **integration**, and **rationale**. Each element requires time and attention to develop. Here's how each impacts the future of your company.

Fit is the connection between parallel company cultures.

Company culture is a powerful force. Culture is how people will act when no one is looking. It specifies the behavior that is tolerated and what gets promoted. A company is a collection of people, and fit simply ensures that the two groups of people involved in the exit share a common set of values around their respective businesses.

A good demonstration of correct fit is the acquisition of Zappos by Amazon. Zappos was known for their customer-obsessed culture. Employees sent handwritten cards, spent hours chatting to a single caller, and even boarded flights to personally deliver packages containing misplaced valuables.[5]

Amazon shared their vision for a customer-first approach to business. They were so well matched that Amazon's Jeff Bezos mentioned he didn't see it as an acquisition. Rather, he said, "I personally would prefer the headline 'Zappos and Amazon sitting in a tree,'" framing the transaction as the beginning of a romantic relationship. He was certainly correct in his assumption that it was the right choice for both cultures.

On the other hand, we've all seen how a bad fit can easily lead to disastrous deals. In 1989, Sony paid $4.8 billion to purchase Columbia Pictures. Sony was a conservative Japanese technology giant, while Columbia Pictures was a fast-paced US-based movie studio. Both companies had completely different operating cultures, and neither side had a plan for how to make them work together. After five years, Sony had written off $3.2 billion of its investment in Columbia Pictures. Not the future any of them wanted.[6]

Cultural fit stems from developing long term relationships. It is extremely important for founders to begin meeting folks in their target companies for this reason. There is a world of difference between an exciting first impression and a relationship of trust that develops over years. It is easy to feign fit in the short term, while it is difficult to maintain long-term.

Alignment means there is agreement among the key people involved in the decision.

It's clear that both parties have multiple stakeholders that need to agree to the transaction. It's important to note that alignment isn't a point in time but an element of the transaction that needs to be maintained. Clear communication, incremental steps to credibility, and, most importantly, mutual trust make up the core components of alignment.

In the following chapters, we will see a master class in alignment in the way Pandora bought Next Big Sound from its CEO, Alex White. While it was Alex's first startup, the board and the shareholders were in lockstep alignment. This was one of the key ingredients that led to a speedy decision and deal execution. We will also learn from serial operator Anne Bonaparte about how she struggled with a rogue board member who wanted to negotiate behind her back with the acquirer.

Founders should first ensure that there is alignment internally, meaning that the four key stakeholders from the startup's perspective are aligned:

- Co-founders
- Board

- Investors
- Executive leadership

We recommend that all startups have an annual "Exit Talk" that acts as a standardized framework to ensure continuous alignment on exit expectations and timing.

Once the internal alignment is there, founders benefit immensely from determining alignment within the acquiring company in parallel.

Integration means there is a clear plan to integrate all elements of the business post-acquisition.

With every deal, the majority of the work that determines if the merger will be successful happens after the documents are signed. This means that there needs to be a plan for integrating everything: people, culture, technology, customer support, parking passes, you name it. Sometimes the task is mundane, like issuing employee IDs, and sometimes the plan is to do nothing.

A successful integration is intentional, with both parties paying attention to details at every step of the way. It is the founders' responsibility to make sure there is a clear plan and purpose around integration, with key metrics to determine success.

We will outline the key steps in an integration journey with examples from companies like Slicehost. When they were acquired by Rackspace, they made sure to communicate the changes to their existing customer base thoughtfully and proactively along the way so existing customer retention wouldn't suffer.

Integrations are difficult, in part because there is so much to do tactically without losing focus on the big picture. It's a complicated process that will generate a lot of questions. The good news is that M&A teams appreciate founders who ask questions about what success looks like post-integration; it tells the acquirer that a founder is serious about creating shared value and getting the deal done. Don't wait until the eleventh hour of negotiations to ask questions around integration. Once you start discussing a term sheet, it is completely standard to ask questions to clarify plans around integration.

A well-crafted integration plan is a critical element of a smooth transaction. Take the time to build it during the closing process, and revisit it post-transaction to ensure mutual accountability.

Rationale is the plan to create new value as a result of the combined capabilities.

This is the final element that determines the success and longevity of an acquisition. A strong rationale is the main ingredient for victory, and a weak one is often the culprit behind deals that end in defeat. The rationale is the core reason behind the acquisition that all parties will align with, and there needs to be a clear business rationale that convincingly predicts an oversized outcome that would not be possible if the two companies remained separate.

The starting point for the rationale is timing. Is now the right time to make this purchase? Is the buyer better off by partnering (becoming a customer or a distributor) or building their own competing product? Timing determines whether an acquisition happens or not. Further, the acquirer will need to have absolute trust in the fundamentals of the business in question.

Trust is created through a credible team, robust technology, and real customers—in other words, you need to create a mountain of evidence to breed confidence in the future plans. Think of this as a basic requirement. In order to even begin discussing a price, you have to be a trustworthy entity.

Assuming that the timing is right and your team is credible, we can answer these critical questions: why should this acquisition happen? What is the mathematical formula of the future value we will create together?

No matter how strategic, at some point in the future, the bill will come due. The acquiring company needs to financially justify their investment in the future. To do this, they design a rationale based on the future success that the two companies will drive together instead of the current performance of their company. Remember that you are selling a vision of the future that happens to be backed up by your credibility.

Founders need to deeply understand the acquirer's business to articulate a defensible rationale.

Facebook knocked this out of the park with its acquisition of Instagram. It was clear that the Facebook team was falling behind on mobile user growth. The tech giant lacked the technology talent and the infrastructure to translate its web-based technology to the growing mobile market. Instagram was clearly ahead, and the rates of growth indicated that each passing day made the budding photo-sharing app more valuable.

The Instagram acquisition is a longer story that we will visit during Part 2, but suffice to say Mark Zuckerberg was initially considered a fool for paying close to $1 billion for the photo-sharing app. Nearly a decade later, Facebook *makes* over $20 billion in ad revenue per year from Instagram, nearly one-fifth of all Facebook revenues.

While Instagram is the crown jewel of Facebook's acquisition portfolio, not every megamerger means a successful future. One of the most visible examples of bad rationale happened in the largest acquisition in tech history: when Time Warner and AOL joined forces. While it made for a good headline, most of the operators working on the deal could not articulate why it made sense for the two companies to join forces.

The rationale is the most critical component of a transaction. Know that as the world changes, so will the rationale. It is critical to build the alignment around the shared objective; this will be the fundamental driver of the transaction.

With a comprehensive understanding of the FAIR framework, plus lessons from those who have successfully (and not so successfully) navigated an exit before you, you are going to make the right exit for you and your company. You'll be able to recognize the elements of FAIR everywhere and use them to create the best future for yourself, your investors, your board, and your employees. Let's begin with the first part of our journey: everything that happens before the company decides to pursue an acquisition.

PART 1

WORKING TOWARD A FAIR ACQUISITION PARTNER

Justin Kan, a successful founder with multiple exits and a partner at YC, sold his first startup, Kiko, on eBay in a process that took less than a week. The final price was $258,100. It was an insanely efficient process in terms of simplicity, but one that failed miserably. He never received the payment and, ultimately, had to shut down his startup.

He later went on to start justin.tv, which became Twitch, the pioneer streaming platform. His exit to

Amazon took much longer than a week, but the final price was much better: $1 billion.

Twitch's success steadily increased after the sale in 2014. It went on to overtake Microsoft's Mixer and delivered more than $2 billion in revenue in 2020. Twitch is a story of how FAIR elements create massive value in the long run. It's not simply because FAIR deals make more money for the founder at the sale (which they do), but they ensure long-term growth and success for everyone as the company becomes even more successful under the parent organization.

How did Justin Kan and Twitch manage to create something so valuable within a larger company? We have to begin by looking many years before the transaction took place. The most successful startup exits are years in the making. An outsized return is only possible by developing foundational trust in the founders, whether through proven reputation or trusted relationships. Both are impossible to generate overnight.

As such, the first part of our journey will focus on that preparation effort: how to sell your company without taking your hands off the wheel.

You might be thinking, *But wait! All of my investors and mentors told me to never worry about the exit. Instead, I should focus on building a great business."* Your mentors are right. You have to ace the fundamentals with your company performance. But you can certainly focus on more than one thing over the next few years.

Somehow, founders accepted that they should spend three to six months every year and a half to fundraise but not even three to six days to work on their eventual acquisition. This is foolish. If you can carve out that time to fundraise, you also have to allocate a smaller amount of time to slowly put together the pieces for your exit. The following chapters will show you how to do that without ever explicitly saying your company is for sale.

You have to get the timing right. Too late, and you lose out on your momentum and face investor fatigue; too early, and you leave money on the table and risk losing investor confidence in your ambition. We will carefully describe the four elements of getting the timing right and what to do before that moment arrives.

A successful exit is about long-term trust, and the key to generating that is empathy. This begins with a deep inspection of your key stakeholders and the folks on the buyer side. Beyond learning their job titles, we will show you how to understand their incentives and make those work for you.

CHAPTER 1

HOW FUNDRAISING IMPACTS THE EXIT

M OST OF US KNOW TRAVIS KALANICK FROM HIS meteoric rise as the CEO of Uber and his ultimate fall from grace. What most don't talk about is his obsessive focus on controlling his own destiny. He had a hard-earned fear of fundraising from his first two startup experiences, and it drove all of his decisions at Uber as well.

Travis began his entrepreneurial journey right before the dot-com boom, with Scour.net. It was an early file-sharing company, a predecessor to Napster. While things got off to a good start, he started having huge issues with Michael Ovitz, his biggest investor. The feared Hollywood executive hung him out to dry when Scour was ultimately sued for $250 billion by entertainment companies for illegal content. Travis was forced to sell, and his investors walked away with all of the proceeds.

It was a devastating outcome that left a deep scar, and he vowed to do things differently next time. He purposefully structured his next company, Red Swoosh, so that he would have control over the exit and, in doing so, managed to walk away with a cool $2 million from the sale to Akamai Technologies.

At Uber, things were no different. He and his partner, Emil Michael, played the game perfectly, wooing investors with their impressive traction. Uber went on to raise billions in capital with a dual stock structure. Pioneered at companies like Facebook and Google, this structure allows common stockholders to have disproportionate voting power in the company. As long as Travis kept his co-founders close, he could do whatever he wanted with more or less impunity. While Uber was able to part ways with him in the end, he walked away with billions.

While he left Uber with billions, Travis paid a heavy price in the decade before starting the company by not carefully managing his cap table. These are costly lessons to learn, and every founder should reflect on their own journey before committing to a decision to fundraise. Before Travis even knew what Uber would be, he solidified his approach to fundraising. He understood the value of a well-established plan as he moved forward in his new company. You need this same understanding before you even think about fundraising, let alone an exit plan. Without it, you'll miss the opportunity to exit the right way, on your terms.

Selling shares in your startup means giving away control of your own destiny. You might still be the CEO, but big decisions like selling your company are now decisions of consensus among you, the board, and your shareholders. This is a bitter pill to swallow, but it is important to begin our conversation with this hard truth: you are no longer fully in charge.

Every decision you make at the beginning will have an impact at the end, including who you will have to listen to when it's time to make big decisions and how the proceeds will ultimately be split. Funding terms you agree to will dictate the equity splits during the exit. How much, under what terms, and from whom you raise capital can mean the difference between a fair exit and one that you feel unhappy about. It could make millions of dollars' worth of difference to your bank account in the end.

We have both learned these lessons personally through failed startups and bitter losses. Each acquisition is unique, but the mistakes we see entrepreneurs repeating are consistent. The lessons around cap table management point to a simple truth: this will take longer than you expected. Forget the mystery phone call you might get one day with someone interested in acquiring you. That happens to some, but it likely won't happen to you. Most acquisitions are priced well under $100 million, and they are the result of a long-term process built on trust.

Every dollar you take and every share you give away matters. The people you decide to take on as investors and shareholders matter.

At this point you need to consider how the equity ownership of your company is distributed. How much do you own? Who else is on the cap table, and under what terms? This information should determine the way you move forward in your fundraising efforts with the exit in mind.

To help get you started on the right path and ensure that you do not make an error early on that causes major ramifications in the future, consider the following six principles for fundraising early on in your journey.

KNOW THYSELF: WHAT KIND OF BUSINESS DO YOU WANT TO BUILD?

Let's begin with the difference between a venture-backable business and a lifestyle business. A venture-backable business is a company whose business model and technology have the potential to generate significantly outsized returns—often one hundred times or more of the valuation of initial investment—fetching valuations above hundreds of millions of dollars.

In contrast, a lifestyle business is a company whose business may be successful, even immensely profitable, but lacks the opportunity to scale above a certain threshold. This may be due to limits in the overall size of the market, growth obstacles around staff and automated systems, or lack of flywheel network effects.

Many first-time entrepreneurs are blind to the important distinctions between these two types of businesses. Just because an entrepreneur is passionate about a given market, idea, or product does not mean it will automatically be venture-backable. There are plenty of examples of companies that need capital to operate but don't find venture investors to be a good fit for their long-term goals. No matter what you decide, you must protect your shares and treat them like the millions of dollars they will be worth in the future.

Above all, make sure that whether you're a venture-backable or lifestyle business, you're staying true to your vision, goals, and mission. Do not try to contort yourself or your company to be palatable for investors. The price of a disingenuous investor relationship is much too steep at the time of exit. You will end up with a company that is unrecognizable to you and a group of people in charge that you do not trust.

A CHANGE IN OWNERSHIP IS A CHANGE IN EXPECTATIONS FOR TIMING OF A LIQUIDITY EVENT

Much of the startup media ecosystem is filled with head-lines covering funding rounds and valuations. While the big numbers are flashy and intriguing, there is much more to fundraising than simply adding capital. It also adjusts the timeline of your future exit. The truth is if you raise money, you're shifting the ownership structure of your business.

Many of the seed stage fundraising terms include pre-ferred shareholders with liquidation preferences. These are the legal rights that determine how the payout from the sale will be distributed. With liquidation preferences, investors can take their money out first, and then the remaining funds are left for distribution.

In addition, it is common to see board structures that favor shareholders instead of the co-founding team. This means that investors can decide to replace you, the CEO, if you disagree with their decision to sell. Conversely, if you are too tired to go on but the company is on a growth path, the board and shareholders can similarly fire the CEO for some-one with higher ambitions for their capital.

This change in ownership comes with an implicit agree-ment and timeline for a liquidity event. Your new co-owner is going to want to come away with a return multiple on that investment on their time horizon, not yours.

This is not inherently a bad thing. In fact, the timeline can work to motivate teams to push toward their goals in efficient and effective ways. However, it is something you need to consider at the very beginning of your entrepreneurial journey. You don't want to be a couple of fundraising rounds into your journey before you understand what your timeline to sale is. You need a plan up front so that you can make intentional decisions that are right for you as soon as possible.

UNDERSTAND HOW MUCH COMMON SHARES ARE WORTH AT WHAT EXIT PRICE

We've been in your shoes, and we interact with entrepreneurs every single day. The truth is that most entrepreneurs are optimizing across the wrong vectors when it comes to fundraising.

Too many founders today are optimizing for the highest valuation, the most money, or the flashiest VC brand to add to their cap table while ignoring the most important key issue: how much are common shares worth when it's time to sell?

By simply prioritizing the highest valuation or the largest amount of funding that can possibly be secured, founders put themselves at risk of erasing any meaningful returns they might receive as a result of the sale. Before you sign a term sheet, you have to know: what will the common shares be worth?

Most founders do not think seriously about the full picture of how those terms will dictate the ways the business will run in the following years or what those terms will mean for an eventual exit. But the amount of money you raise, the source of that capital, and the valuation at which the funding is secured determine the waterfall: the distribution of the proceeds.

Most entrepreneurs are familiar with the VC model. VCs will make ten bets in the hope that one or two will be "home runs" and return ten times the value of the investment. To further remove risks from their investments, many carve out preferred shares that pay back before common stock, occasionally with a multiple attached to the preference. In practical terms, an investor might be guaranteed a 3x return before any of the proceeds are available for the rest of the shareholders, including you and your team. If the price of the exit is only 2x what they paid for the company and the investor was guaranteed 3x, then all of the proceeds will go to the investors.

In the simplest terms, you are giving up a portion of the equity ownership in your company for money, but that money can come at a great price. It comes with financial and legal obligations that tie your fate and that of your company to a third-party investor. You need to be sure that the money you are "buying" will be worth it—and that there will be something left over for you and your employees at the end. A well-structured fundraise and sensible valuations mean that you will walk away rich when the dust settles. A rushed process and tough terms on the exit in exchange for a flashy valuation could mean that you walk away with nothing.

We understand the temptation. It feels great to read a TechCrunch article that features your company's accomplishments, including funding from a top venture fund. The same teams that once backed giants like Google, Facebook, and Amazon are now betting on your success. This is a great feeling, but one that can lead founders to lose sight of what they are giving up. Consider yourself in the shoes of a CEO who is looking at three term sheets for an upcoming round:

1. A brand-name VC firm at a high valuation with an associate in a board observer role.
2. A midsize venture fund at a lower valuation that would dedicate personal time and with a valuable network.
3. Two older, very experienced angel operators with an even lower valuation who would dedicate one day per week in service of the company.

These are vastly different offers, and the unique benefits and downsides of each structure are much more important than the economics.

The first scenario is best for founders who are seasoned, understand the market they are going after, and don't need much help or guidance from their shareholders. An associate in that fund is likely to get experience as an observer and junior voice on the board, and experienced founders know how to manage the rest of their boards. Practically speaking, a higher valuation coupled with passive investors is not always a bad combination. As long as you are confident that there is a direct path to victory, this is a straightforward choice to make.

The second scenario is for founders who will need more capital down the road. A seasoned VC who has been in operator roles will be an invaluable member of the board and can offer practical advice on most issues surrounding the CEO. Mark is one of those VCs, someone who holds you to high standards and outcomes while approaching issues with empathy and a give-first mentality.

Additionally, access to the network a VC like this has will make the rest of the fundraising process much more efficient. A warm introduction from someone who has made money for them in the past does wonders for making a successful first conversation. You should use it to your advantage.

The slight increase in the equity you give away now will return itself many times over in future rounds. This was the situation for Cameo and its Chicago-based founder, Steven Galanis. Ezra Galston from Chicago Ventures led his seed round with a modest $3.2 million check. He was shortly followed by Pritzker Group Venture Capital with a $12.5 million investment. Nine months later, Kleiner Perkins led the series B with a $50 million check at a reported $300 million in valuation. None of that would have been possible without Ezra's first check.

The final scenario is the most complicated one, and it really depends on a single factor: how good are the operators joining the management team for one day per week? The right mentor—one who is willing to take you under their wing and give you real support—will accelerate your development as a CEO. The return on this can't be measured with the percentage of the company you are giving up.

It is extremely difficult to determine if the partners in front of you can give you the kind of guidance you need, but that is where their track record working with founders comes in. Do your research, and never make a decision that doesn't align with your core values and motivations. For a first-time founder, this may be a particularly important choice to consider. Moreover, if the company is poised for profitability and you intend to grow with your own profits, having a steady hand at the helm is more critical than your ability to raise capital.

A seasoned VC can teach you how to fundraise. A seasoned operator will teach you how to run a company with solid fundamentals. Additional capital can mask issues, and no junior MBA can give you a parallel experience to learning from the best.

YOU SHOULD CONDUCT DUE DILIGENCE ON YOUR INVESTORS

Fundraising feels like an accomplishment. And it certainly is. You have managed to successfully sell shares in your company—a great vote of confidence in your future success.

When it is all said and done, it feels great to see the wires come in. The horizon is bright, and the resource cabinet is stocked for the adventures ahead.

But don't let the promise of a champagne toast over-shadow the responsibility of the founders to do their home-work. Both the founders and investors need to ensure they are making the right decision. Investors are professionals at this—they invest capital for a living and know the red flags to look out for. Just like when your company is being acquired, the odds are stacked against you.

Your job is to suss out the red flags of your potential inves-tors. Treat it like a true partnership. Remember you are hir-ing them to provide capital for your future. Not doing real, substantive due diligence can be disastrous, even for the most experienced operators.

Gregg Kaplan is a well-known Chicago-area entrepreneur who started Redbox out of the innovation department of McDonalds and grew it to a more than $2 billion annual sales company in just seven years. He then founded Swing King and Modjule and became an operating partner at Pritzker Group Venture Capital. He has been through the trenches and has learned the lessons of picking the wrong partners over the years.

He advised that above and beyond the percentage of the company you are giving away, you first need to define the rela-tionship between the two parties. "There are a lot of investors who are looking to get the best deal for themselves, not for all parties involved. It's incredibly hard to discern the real character of someone before the critical moment of a transaction," he said. To Gregg, the real character of your future partner shows up in their behavior during the raise and, if left unaddressed, comes back to haunt you during the exit.

For him, this means only doing business with known quantities—a luxury that seasoned operators may have but is not a realistic standard for most founders. So what can founders do to mitigate their risk instead of simply hoping their investors turn out to be nice people?

Taking someone's money should be treated like a job interview. *You* are interviewing *them* to see if you want to take their money. Another way to think about it is that you are buying their investment, and you need to read the fine print.

Request lots of information. Ask for their full list of CEOs and phone numbers. Ask what their returns are like. Reach out to their co-investors who serve on mutual boards. Talk to the companies that have exited in their portfolio. Don't just talk to the flashy exits. Find the founders who barely returned 1–2x paid-in capital.

Any hesitancy on the part of an investor to freely provide this information once requested is a red flag. If they have good outcomes and good relationships with their portfolio founders, it should be no problem to provide it.

As an active investor over decades, Mark has created his own no-fly list for investors he stays away from working with.

These are individuals who spur infighting among shareholders, make eleventh-hour demands, or immediately resort to legal action every time they don't get their way. In other words, folks who view the world as a zero-sum game. Folks who believe "you have to lose in order for me to win."

Those individuals on the no-fly list generally assume that they are doing right by their investors (the limited partners of their funds). In reality, they are winning a few short term points while losing out on their reputation. If you are known to be a difficult entity to work with, you will be left out of future term sheets.

Look, we get it; sometimes your back is up against the wall, and you might not have an alternative path to raising capital. But nothing sucks the joy out of life like a bad partner. A slight bank account may be bad; we guarantee you that having the wrong partner will eventually be worse.

EVERY SHARE COUNTS, SO AVOID "DEAD EQUITY" ON THE CAP TABLE

At the outset, cap table management is one of the most important decisions you have to make. Aside from selling shares to raise funds, there are other ways founders give up equity in their companies.

To whom you decide to give shares is one of the most consequential matters in this process. How much are you going to give to co-founders? How much do you set aside for employee options? Who will serve on your board and at what price?

It's imperative to limit the amount of "dead equity" you have on your books. Dead equity is the number of shares given away to people who are not actively building the value of your company. Be stingy with it because every share matters in the end. The best operators ensure that every share of equity goes to people who are making that success possible.

But too often, founders give away too much stock up front, whether to early partners, employees, or advisors. Let's take a closer look at what some mistakes might look like.

A founder who is no longer there. Imagine that three business school classmates decide to start a business. They each work equally to get it off the ground and split the company ownership evenly in thirds. Then two of the three decide they want to stick with it full time. The third needs one of those pesky "real jobs."

Because of the initial company structure, and assuming it hasn't changed, that third individual will continue to own a third of the company even without their full commitment and input. This will stick out like a sore thumb down the road. They might have blocking rights to a sale, and they will do exactly that if they have a grudge against the team that stayed behind. Typically, co-founder dramas end ugly, no matter who is right.

Think about what it would feel like to lose out on a life-changing transaction because someone had an axe to grind. That's why terms like stock vesting schedules and cliffs are crucial. Don't just give away big chunks of the company without solidifying the terms required to vest the stock.

The best way to deal with this problem is to avoid having it in the first place. As soon as you have an idea, get a lawyer to spend an hour with you on a very straightforward vesting schedule. A one-year cliff and four-year vesting is market standard—it means that employees must stay with the company for a full year to claim 25 percent of their equity. If they meet that threshold, the rest will start accruing monthly until they accrue all their equity in a total of four years.

An early "advisor" who no longer adds value. Advisors who demand unconscionable amounts of equity only to vanish without delivering real value are another common culprit of dead equity. These types of startup hangers-on often give very tempting pitches and lead founders to believe they have the answer to every problem or the keys to early sales growth.

We have all been intoxicated with the promises of what an amazing advisor can do for our company. Unfortunately, more often than not, these are dreams, not reality. Be extremely wary of any advisor who asks for a chunk of equity up front before they've proven the value they are going to add. If someone has made ten warm introductions that led to new sales, this dynamic is entirely different. Raise your bar before you commit to an advisor, especially with equity.

THE AMOUNT OF THE RAISE, SOURCE OF CAPITAL, AND VALUATION/TERMS DETERMINE THE WATERFALL: THE DISTRIBUTION OF THE PROCEEDS

Hopefully, you've taken all of this into consideration and found wonderful partners to grow your business with. Don't worry; there are multiple paths for you and your team to have a great outcome.

Let's evaluate the most important document: the waterfall. This is the spreadsheet that will change your life, where your sweat and equity transform into capital. The waterfall is sometimes referred to as the preference stack, the order in which shareholders receive their money. This is an even bigger deal if the final price of the company doesn't meet valuation targets.

In order to understand this, there are three examples on the following page of how the chips would fall in relatively similar transactions.

The first scenario is the simplest. You have used your own source of capital or, even better, the revenues from your customers to grow your business. This means that you are in total control of the time and distribution; you get to call the shots. The final price of $30 million is completely yours, minus the share to Uncle Sam.

Company sells for $30,000,000

	Scenario 1	Scenario 2	Scenario 3	Scenario 4
Capital Raised	–	$2,000,000	$10,000,000	$10,000,000
Preference		1x	1x	2x participating
Pre-Money Valuation		$8,000,000	$15,000,000	$15,000,000
Post-Money Valuation		$10,000,000	$25,000,000	$25,000,000
Entrep. %	100%	80%	60%	60%
Investor %		20%	40%	40%
Preference				$20,000,000
Entrep. $	$30,000,000	$24,000,000	$18,000,000	$6,000,000
Investor $		$6,000,000	$12,000,000	$24,000,000

In the second scenario, the company has sold one-fifth of their company, and the resulting exit meant that the entrepreneur made a cool $24 million in the exit before tax. This is directly proportional and would be considered a great outcome.

The third scenario had more capital invested and a higher valuation! The headline version of this exit would certainly read better, but the bill will come due for the founder in the end. The larger sale of the shares means that the founder is down to $18 million. Still, not bad.

However, the final scenario is where the preference stack rears its ugly head. Imagine the same dollars in Scenario 3 but with the simple addition of a 2x preference stack with participating preferred shares. (This wouldn't even make it to the TechCrunch article; the hyped-up valuation reads the same!) In the waterfall, this means the investors can take out their investment at a 2x return first, prior to the proceeds to all of the shareholders. This guarantees $20 million in return, and the remaining funds are divided up according to shareholder percentages. Suddenly, the investors have turned the tides—founders are only walking away with $6 million. This is a material difference and should be a cautionary tale to pay really close attention to all of the terms you are signing up for during fundraising.

While raising capital is an important factor, selling your company is an awesome thing.

If you make the right calls, you can walk away with a life-changing sum of money as a result of all of this planning and intentional fundraising and decision-making. It is extremely exciting to see the dream you poured years of your life into reach even bigger heights.

As long as founders pay close attention to their partnerships, develop sound operating principles, and prepare themselves for a FAIR exit, things will work out. In the end, all shareholders, including both common and preferred shareholders, want the highest return possible. While the investment terms dictate the distribution, whether the transaction happens or not depends on an entirely different currency: trust. In the next chapter, we will dig into how trust factors into the sale of your company.

CHAPTER 2

BUILDING TRUST TAKES TIME

THINK ABOUT THE LIST OF PEOPLE YOU TRUST THE most. These can be family members, romantic partners, and, hopefully, your close business relationships. The common thread with those people should be evident:

1. Trust took a long time to form.
2. You have overcome challenges together, not just celebrated good times.
3. You have grown to respect their judgment in key decisions.

Now put yourself in the shoes of an acquiring company. These same themes would show up with the companies you were considering as potential partners. For most startups, the values of the organization reflect the values of the CEO, and the trust you build around yourself as the leader will reflect the value for the rest of the organization.

We know that selling your company begins with the decisions made during fundraising. That defines the loose architecture around value and timing. However, the fuel that powers a FAIR exit is trust between leaders. It is the single biggest asset that you can have as a CEO. There is a tremendous amount of goodwill required for a transaction to happen, and a dearth of trust will make the sale dead on arrival. The good news is you can start building this trust with everyone you know immediately.

Before we dive into how to build the necessary trust and relationships, let's pause to clarify a point. What makes an exit possible is a sound business with great fundamentals. You need to exceed tremendous expectations and prove the value of your technology, product, customer base—whatever it is that makes your company unique. Without building and proving significant market value, you can't expect to see an offer at all, much less a FAIR one.

One of the common pieces of pushback we received from our colleagues in writing this book was a protest: "Just hunker down and build a great business; a buyer will show up!" To that we say, *"Yes, and..."* Of course you have to hunker down and build a great business, but you also need to be aware of how your early decisions and ability to establish relationships will ultimately determine your outcomes.

What we are describing here is an efficient way to run a silent process in the background, to build layers of trust and authentic relationships over time, so that you are "selling" your company well in advance of when the actual deal process begins. The advice in this chapter about building and banking trust is intended to foster the dynamics that lead to successful, well-valued sales with as little friction as possible. After all, it is much easier to build a huge castle on a solid foundation.

A successful exit doesn't happen by accident. You want your company to be valued on what it can do with the parent company. The only way that will happen is if you have a deep understanding of what the companies can accomplish under one umbrella.

STARTUPS NEED TO BANK A LOT OF TRUST BEFORE A SUCCESSFUL TRANSACTION

Exits are hard, primarily for three reasons:

There is too much to do. There are lots of variables to focus on. From simple relationship building to complicated due diligence, getting acquired takes a lot of effort. Founders are stuck between focusing on getting the exit right and operating their companies smoothly so they continue to hit their targets.

Focus is extremely important when time is limited, and a startup can easily lose it with the shiny allure of a successful payout. This leads to competing objectives: if the acquiring company really cares about sales performance but does not care about product development, the company might focus on what matters to the buyer instead of the organization or the customer.

In addition, if the deal falls apart—which happens more often than a successful transaction—this can be a massive time sink for the organization as a whole. Those lost months do not come back. And at that point you're facing sinking morale from a team stung by defeat.

Right before your exit is not the time to add a complex task to your to-do list. Even if it were possible to establish genuine trust, there wouldn't be enough time to juggle that along with all your other responsibilities. That's why building trust is a long-term goal you need at the very beginning.

There are too many stakeholders. CEOs need to align (and then keep aligning) a large group of competing stakeholders while negotiating an exit. You can expect to manage everyone from your internal investor base, the board of directors, and the leadership team to external stakeholders like legal teams, bankers, and executives who are both working for and against your acquisition. Each individual stakeholder creates a new relationship of trust you need to build and maintain.

As such, spreading these responsibilities over time will make it easier for you to focus on the top priorities of each stakeholder. You won't be scrambling to understand each person's goals while trying to execute a sale. You'll already have a clear picture based on numerous conversations over time.

There is too much on the line. Exits are life-changing. A transaction can lead to generational wealth, a healthier lifestyle, a wider network of mentors for your future, and a mission far greater than what the startup could accomplish on its own. Because so much is on the line, it can be increasingly difficult to operate under pressure.

The price of a mistake during the regular course of a startup can be high, but it is rarely critical. Companies typically do not go out of business because of one blunder. However, in an M&A process, a deal can fall apart immediately after one wrong phone call, one meeting that goes awry, or one diligence item that does not add up. Without built-in trust, there is no way to recover from an inevitable challenging moment.

It takes nerves of steel to maintain a steady hand throughout all of this. Trust is the solution; it eases your stress and the buyer's checkbook.

EVALUATING TRUST WITH DIFFERENT STAKEHOLDERS: BOARD, INVESTORS, INTERNAL LEADERSHIP TEAM

Key leadership needs to remain focused on execution during the sale.

When the moment to sell arrives, you will need key employees on your side. They will need to trust you that you have their back—that they will be taken care of with compensation or through a new role in their new home.

We will dig into the details of the need for transparency about the upcoming transaction in later chapters, but the broader point is simple: if you have been a tyrant, an abusive leader who took advantage of your team to get here, the bill will come due.

You need extreme alignment and loyalty among your team as you present your company to an acquirer. If there is mutiny on board, the turmoil will show up as bad performance. No buyer wants to inherit a crisis, and if the team doesn't trust you are doing right by them, they won't stand by you.

The **Board of Directors** builds credibility and trust in the judgment of the CEO.

Laying the groundwork for a positive transaction experience starts with cultivating trust with your board. Developing trust means developing relationships. And developing relationships means focusing on communication.

If your board members trust you, they trust your judgment. With that trust, they will likely embrace your reasoning and your decision to sell with enthusiasm.

Don't simply rely on quarterly meetings and long decks to create trust. Commit to what you can deliver, and show up with results. Especially during the sale process, make sure you are scheduling regular one-on-one check-ins with each individual. Your board needs to know what's going on, where you are experiencing challenges, and what your plans are to face those challenges. Board alignment is your responsibility; remember that the sale is only in consideration because the board decided to consider it.

Alex White, the Founder and CEO of Next Big Sound, sold his company to Pandora in 2015. It was his first transaction. Alex did a lot of things right, but he also made some mistakes because he was a first-time founder. One of the benefits of collecting industry wisdom in a book like this is that now a bigger audience can learn from the mistakes that others have made.

One of the things Alex got right was the trust he was able to secure from his board. Brad Navin was an independent board member of Next Big Sound and the CEO of the Orchard, a music label owned by Sony. A great operator in his own right, Brad led the acquisition of the Orchard to Sony. Afterword, as one of the key leaders at the mega-label, he led dozens of acquisitions. He recalled that one of the things that stood out to him was Alex's very careful cultivation of meaningful relationships with each individual board member. "He did all of the right things with the board, and when it came time to ask us for the vote, there was no question in anyone's mind."

The more trust you bank, the less alignment you will need internally.

Investors (your shareholders) need to align behind the board's final decision and need to trust your word that this is the best direction.

Chances are that your investors trust you a great deal already. After all, they trusted millions of their hard-earned dollars to your care. Regular monthly updates on your traction and challenges are a must to avoid losing this trust and maintain enthusiasm for your vision.

Your investors have already likely modeled out what your company could be worth one day. It is imperative to understand these expectations and make sure that the offer you bring to the table clears their return expectations. There are no issues if you come with an offer that exceeds expectations. No one complains about winning the lottery. The problem is what happens if you are delivering an offer below expectations because they still need to approve your decision to sell.

Investors need to sign off on your deal to proceed, period. The way you carry their trust during these challenging moments will guarantee their ultimate decision to support you and their decision to back your next company.

HAVE AN ANNUAL EXIT TALK WITH THE BOARD TO SET AND MAINTAIN EXPECTATIONS AND BUILD CREDIBILITY AND TRUST

The foundation of all trust is open communication. We all know this instinctively, but we tend to forget it when we get busy. We prioritize other issues and forget to stay in regular communication with the important stakeholders in our organization. But you need to talk about selling your company with your stakeholders often and consistently. Getting acquired is not a bad thing, after all—a successful exit is the desired outcome for most startups. What hurts is when the acquisition is a surprise—a distraction from the shared commitment everyone is there for.

Start a conversation about selling too early, and the shareholders will doubt the long-term commitment of the leadership. Too resistant to a sale, and the shareholders will grow frustrated with their expectations for a positive return. This is a tough balancing act, but it should not prevent you from discussing an exit at all.

Unfortunately, the conventional wisdom is for founders to virtually never discuss exits with shareholders. It is frowned upon to talk about the sale—investors expect the founders to constantly be focused on building an even bigger company until they are ready to cash out. The challenge is that if the founders are bringing up the sale conversation, it looks like they are interested in selling the company before the maximum value can be achieved. In other words, the board will question the long-term commitment of the CEO if the conversation comes up prematurely.

Founders need to establish the expectation with their boards that once a year, the group will add an agenda item to the meeting related to the sale. It is simply a temperature check on long-term strategy, potential strategic buyers, and time horizons. This will allow you to build rapport, continue the process of alignment, and establish the trust you need to have a FAIR deal. The exit is one of the most important moments in the life of a startup for the founders and investors alike. A conversation filled with anxiety, doubt, and mistrust serves no one. Carving out intentional space to have these conversations in an open and honest fashion on a periodic basis will improve outcomes for all parties.

The secret to board (and shareholder) buy-in is consistent communication on expectations and strategy to achieve objectives. This is where the CEO can withdraw from the trust bank that they have been putting the savings in over the years with their consistent communication.

The goal of these conversations is not to kick off a sale but to ensure there is alignment around key questions:

- What is our threshold walk-away price?
- What is the fund timeline to return proceeds for limited partners?

- What objectives need to be accomplished for existing investors to further capitalize the company?
- Who are the key buyers, old and new? With whom should the CEO be building relationships in those companies?
- What is the key performance metric those buyers care about? What is the strategy to optimize that further?

We call this the *Exit Talk*: a key ingredient for a successful exit and effective governance. It is also an opportunity for a CEO to educate their shareholders and board on what matters. These are the moments to build shareholder confidence, define what the possible exit may look like, and execute on that premise.

It is true that if a founder never mentions a sale for eight years and suddenly starts bringing up the topic to a board, it signals a lack of energy to win even bigger. The reverse is also true: VCs are managing a fund with return expectations. A founder unaware of the dynamics of the investors and their timeline doesn't help the anxiety surrounding the sale.

Instead of fueling the awkwardness of the exit topic by staying silent, we are putting forward a new norm that we believe the entire industry should adopt: the Exit Talk.

The moment the founder shakes hands with the investor who will join the board, they should agree to bring up this question once a year: are we ready to sell our company? In most cases, the answer will be a simple no—but the space itself will take out the anxiety that a founder will feel when they bring up this question. This is one of the many norms we hope to shift in the world of startups today in order to take the stigma out of this important conversation.

In addition to the board, regular check-ins (about once a year is the right cadence) with the core leadership team to update them on the current thinking surrounding an exit are similarly beneficial. Take the temperature of your team, and fill them in on where your head is. Is everybody still in the game? Are there things you should be worried about? Is this the right time to sell? Use correct judgment, and limit the discussion to your top leadership, but be honest and transparent with the folks who will take the company to its ultimate destination. If the ultimate goal is to go public, you need to have extreme dedication from your key leadership to stick it out long term, not just from the founders.

DEVELOP A BUYER ECOSYSTEM EARLY

In 2015, Paul Graham, the YC founder, penned a controversial essay, "Don't Talk to Corp Dev." In it, he makes the case that thinking about exits distracts from growth and it's not helpful to have early conversations with your competition or larger companies in your industry. In the worst-case scenario, your competition could even steal your idea.

This kind of thinking pushes founders to the extremes. The exit becomes a mythical, winning-the-lottery-type event (with similar odds and returns), or the company goes out of business through a stress sale.

It's just not how things work in the real world. It won't help your business be successful in its own right, and it definitely won't help you achieve a satisfying exit outcome. A FAIR deal requires long-term relationships and mutual trust. The acquirer needs to trust the projections based on past performance and current momentum. Paul Graham's advice is just not practical for most startups; CEOs need to start building relationships early.

Think of your relationships with corporate development as similar to VCs. You don't rely on these relationships to run your business, but it helps to keep the lines of conversation open. After all, an acquisition is basically a mega funding round with a much longer timeline.

Anne Bonaparte is a seasoned technology CEO who has successfully navigated eight acquisitions. She has spent decades in the startup ecosystem and has tremendous wisdom in the art of identifying a key asset in whatever industry she becomes a part of.

One of the first things she does when she assumes the leadership position is reach out to competitors, potential acquirers, or strategic partners. Whether it is sharing the latest industry trends, future regulatory changes, or potential shared customers, she always has a pulse on what the industry values the most.

As she stressed to us, "You want to be known."

This is the exact kind of activity that needs time, like building your reputation. Mark learned this lesson when it came time to sell his first company, the Whitewater Group. It had been seven years. The company was growing, but slowly. This was purgatory for the VCs, and they were getting restless. Mark made it a habit to reach out to the CEOs of his competitors and develop good relations and open lines of communication. He particularly focused on Gordon Eubanks, then-CEO of Symantec. Every time he went to the Valley, he made sure to stop in and say hi to Gordon. Over the years they developed a trusted relationship. When it came time to sell the company, it was easy for Gordon to say yes.

Experienced CEOs have an idea of the potential buyers of their startup before they launch. In most marketplaces, there are usually a handful of Fortune 500 competitors, followed by a number of up-and-coming upstarts and dozens of early-stage startups. For most, the top prospects will come from the large Fortune 500s. But it's also good to keep an eye on the fact that increasingly more financial buyers from traditional private equity firms are moving down-market to invest in technology companies.

You can easily find out online who the key executives are, from the CEO down to the M&A leadership. Reach out to them. As Anne says, make yourself a known entity. Touch base with them once or twice a year. If you have trade shows or large conferences, squeeze in a dinner or lunch meeting.

A CEO who is not cultivating these personal relationships is a CEO who is putting a ceiling on future value. The single largest currency in every M&A transaction is trust. And to earn trust, you must give it first. It takes years for people to know who you are, what your company does, and, most importantly, your trajectory for the road ahead. The reason technology companies command many multiples on their current revenues or enterprise value is not because of where they are but where they are going.

The trust investments you are making along the way should lead to an ecosystem of buyers, each representing a unique vision for the future. Think of this as an exploration of what the future could ultimately be—it's an engaging thought experiment to imagine what could be possible with the resources of a huge company like Google.

The time to start building that relationship is now. Your historical financial reports, company presentations, and news releases all serve to establish credibility for your future projections. However, it is very difficult to establish you, the founder, as trustworthy as a result of a one-hour meeting. Knowing your buyers personally and keeping them abreast of your progress gives them confidence to trust you when it counts the most.

Depending on the size of your exit, this buyer network is one of the values of having experienced bankers on your side. However, there is nothing that can replace the personal credibility a founder can bring to the table. Conversely, if your reputation is tainted among your competitors or your buyers, the sale is over before it begins.

Trust is also built indirectly. CEOs need to be part of the influencer ecosystem that the buyer follows: press, analysts, professional organizations, conferences, and more. Pair a trustworthy persona with a genuine relationship, and the buyers will line up to work with you. In some cases, time is even a critical ingredient in and of itself.

INCREMENTAL STEPS TO CREDIBILITY LEAD TO FUTURE DECISIONS MADE WITH CONFIDENCE

Even if built over years, trust still needs to be maintained throughout the thick of the sale process. Each interaction with the buyer—now much more frequent—should lead to a higher degree of trust.

When a major customer has a multiyear contract with their signature on it, your future revenue growth will be more credible. When the buyers evaluate your turnover rate over the years, they will understand that you have a tight-knit team that has each other's backs. Familiar investors on your cap table will breed further trust that they are on the right track to work with you.

Remember, the final contract of a sale is ultimately a fancy employment agreement for you. They are deciding to work with you and invest a ton of resources to make that happen. People don't work with people they don't trust. Just like the buyer, you need to feel great about your new home, and trust is the most important ingredient.

Each side can afford a few backward steps if you are starting from a foundation of trust and respect. Once you have built this up, you still need to decide when the timing is right.

CHAPTER 3

WHEN IS THE RIGHT TIME TO BEGIN THE ACTUAL PROCESS OF A SALE?

K NOWING WHEN TO TRANSITION FROM CASUAL conversations and relationship building to a more purposeful process driven by urgency is a critical skill for every CEO.

Ideally, the decision to initiate a serious sales process originates from the startup CEO as a result of long-term planning efforts. Whether peaceful or contentious, a startup cannot be sold with a leader who doesn't want the transaction to happen.

A startup that has raised investor dollars is a startup that's for sale. Whether the leader is supportive or contentious about the decision, a sale is the intended destination for a company that has done any fundraising. Hopefully, you have already considered the expectations and timeline of your investors for a liquidity event and have been building and banking trust with your investors, board, key employees, and the industry partners who will form the base of your likely acquirers.

A transaction can only happen when an acquirer is willing to pay a premium on the current value of a business. The amount of that premium—one that aligns everyone around a decision—is the key detail to define.

This is paramount. A responsible board will swiftly replace a CEO who wants to sell the company before investors are ready to sell or one who is blocking a sale that the investors are eager to proceed with. While an exit can be an awesome event, it can also be the very reason that the CEO gets fired.

If things go according to plan, the trigger event is not reactionary. Ideally, the decision will be made proactively as part of a broader set of actions, including building long-term relationships, creating an ecosystem of buyers, and stacking the team in your favor.

When a CEO is forced to sell the company, that is the wrong time to sell. There are a number of situations that force a sale; the most typical one is running out of capital and not being able to raise more. Dubbed an asset sale, it means that the investors and the team were forced to liquidate the company. If the alternative is to go out of business, the buyer has all the leverage in the world and will squeeze the process all the way to the end to secure the minimum price. This is not a recipe for success in either the short or long term.

Remember that no matter how many planning and negotiation skills this book teaches you, the company must be performing in order to have a successful exit. Now, assuming that the company is crushing its key objectives, it is time to pull the trigger to kick off an exit process.

This chapter will put a lens on that trigger moment: when to make the call to sell. How can a CEO know that it is the right time?

WHAT KIND OF SALE IS THIS?

The typical image that comes to mind when a startup is acquired is similar to a spaceship docking to a space station. There is a much larger, more established company that the startup engages with and eventually gets permanently tied to. But this isn't always the case.

There are essentially four kinds of buyers of technology startups.

The first is a **financial buyer**. These are entities that buy all or a significant portion of the company during an early liquidity event. Typically, a financial buyer is a private equity fund or a late-stage investor. There is no strategic alignment necessary here. More often than not, a PE fund that specializes in a market will look for a 2–3x return in four to eight years, depending on the fund size and dynamics. They take on significantly less risk than a venture capitalist, hence the need to buy out the existing shareholders.

Such was the case with Emmi Solutions, a healthcare technology startup from Chicago where Mark held a seat on the board. Founded in 2002, the company had raised $15 million in venture financing when it was recapitalized by Primus Ventures in 2013 at a $70 million valuation. Some of the existing investors cashed out at that price, with an acceptable return. A majority of the investors kept their shares as they approved the new direction. This greatly simplified the cap table, which was flooded with smaller investors that would have made a healthy acquisition virtually impossible. With new leadership and fresh capital, the company crushed its sales objectives and was eventually acquired by Wolters Kluwer in 2016 for $170 million in an all-cash deal.

Not every financial buyer is a positive return for shareholders. Especially when the company needs a fresh start, financial buyers can introduce significant downsides. For example, a recapitalization event (also known as a recap) essentially replaces the existing set of investors by diluting the existing shareholders. Usually, this happens when the company genuinely found its footing, albeit a little later than the time frame that the early shareholders or the founding executive team predicted. Financial buyers of established companies may also borrow a significant amount of money, "or leverage," to make the transaction. This debt load becomes part of the company and can be a significant drag on profitability.

An alternative to a recap is known as a rollup, where the PE fund will acquire adjacent companies to create a platform of services. This is an effort to integrate a number of businesses to create end-to-end solutions that carry a premium. For instance, imagine an online food-ordering application, a menu-scraping tool, and a delivery fleet coming together to build Uber Eats.

There are exceptions in every case, but a private equity fund's main objective is to acquire an ownership position in an already established business and further the profitability of the company by streamlining the operations. The existing leadership team (including the founders) is typically replaced with a new group of leaders to make that happen, which means it's not always the right answer for companies.

Those who don't want a financial buyer may consider a **competitive buyer**. In markets where two companies with similar products compete head-to-head with similar services, one company can purchase the other to increase their market share. Typically, this is not an ideal outcome financially, as it means that one side won.

While the financial return is likely not great, this is a very smooth process since the integration is much easier. The buyer knows where the employees belong in the parent company and is able to serve the existing set of customers with a similar service.

Founders may also consider **public buyers**, where the broader public buys small pieces of the company during its initial public offering. This is still very much a liquidation event; however, it does not result in a change in the direction of the company. Instead, it is a vote of confidence in the existing momentum of the company. While there are always cases of activist investors who want to alter that trajectory, more often than not, a retail investor is simply looking to make a decent return by buying low and selling high.

A very small percentage of technology companies that are successful end up going public. It is a significant liquidity event for virtually all shareholders.

Lastly, we have **strategic buyers**. This is the spaceship we want to dock in. The best kind of buyer, these are usually opportunistic, larger companies looking to further their goals exponentially with the acquisition.

Getting acquired by a strategic buyer could mean an increase to your bottom line, competitive access to key customers, a stronger technological advantage, and more. In short, this is likely the most lucrative financial outcome. The buyer isn't purchasing the company's assets as is; they are purchasing the company's potential impact on the much bigger company. For example, a 10 percent lift for McDonald's sales is worth billions, and if the startup can make a legitimate case for how their technology can accomplish that, they will drive the price up. The best-case scenario is that there are a handful of strategic buyers that your startup can add value to.

WHAT ARE YOU SELLING? DEFINE YOUR KEY ASSET

When you determine to whom you're going to sell, it's important to focus on what you're selling so that you know exactly how to position yourself to the right buyers. Every buyer has a "key value" in mind when they consider acquiring a company. This doesn't mean that the rest of the company's performance is negligible, but there is always one metric that matters more than others.

To identify what that is, we begin with empathy toward the objectives of the buyers. By clearly knowing who the buyers are, we can also start discovering what they value the most. A competitor that is focused on gaining more market share will put less value on your EBITDA than a protected technical edge. Certain companies care about IP; others care about speed of innovation. Your buyer might be playing defense for protecting their sales instead of fighting for new customers. The kind of value an acquisition can bring varies, but it is quantifiable and something you should work to understand in each sale. Remember when analysts were baffled by Facebook's purchase of Instagram for nearly $1 billion? All they saw was a company that barely made any meaningful money being gobbled up for way too much. They failed to see what Mark Zuckerberg saw. They didn't know how Instagram had positioned themselves to fulfill a need he had for Facebook. And now, Instagram is estimated to be worth $100 billion within the walls of Facebook.

A seasoned CEO will know what they are selling. Optimizing this asset—whether it is your costs, growth rates, profits, or talent—should be your top priority before the trigger is pulled. For instance, if your top metric is growth rates in users, you need to start improving that to a predictable cadence three to four years in a row prior to a sale. This furthers your ability to forecast into the future and secure a price based on what will happen. If you get this right, the key asset becomes the core of the rationale behind the acquisition.

THE KEY MOMENT: THE LOCAL MAXIMUM

Once a CEO understands what they are selling and to whom they are selling it, the question of when exactly to sell becomes much clearer. We call this the local maximum: there is increasing momentum for our key asset, but there are challenges on the horizon that will need time and resources to overcome.

For Alex White, the CEO of Next Big Sound, this moment materialized in January 2015, when one of his competitors was acquired by Apple. In a limited world of acquirers, taking a major player off the table is always a scary moment. It had been seven years since he founded the company, and he was struggling to find the motivation and positive growth outlook to push further. The acquisition of their competitor, coupled with likely having to raise a series B in nine months when they still didn't have a repeatable, scalable sales playbook, was a lot to face! Looking back, he acknowledged, "I was exhausted. And it was a very draining and isolating time because I felt like I couldn't talk to anyone about wanting to sell."

He continued, "I knew this was as good a time as any to explore selling the company. I knew it was our local maximum moment. In February 2015, Next Big Sound was named by *Fast Company* as the most innovative company in the music industry and to their top-50 list of most innovative companies in the world. This was our best chance to have the best outcome for my team and investors."

Seasoned executive teams can anticipate the obstacles in front of them, even when everything appears to be meeting expectations. They can read the signs from the future and make decisions about their local maximum. Perhaps conversion rates are going down, customer acquisition costs are going up, new competitors are entering the market, or something even smaller. This is not the same thing as momentum dying. These are cases where the leadership team is aware and can articulate what needs to be overcome to grow even more. This nuance is the difference between a strategic acquisition and an asset sale that is spiraling toward an eventual death.

The local maximum is a moment in your timeline when the valuation for the company is confidently based on your trajectory in spite of the challenges ahead. This is the best time to sell your startup.

In any transaction, you are essentially trading your hard work for what the market is willing to pay. Your progress to date, cash in the bank, and sales momentum are all easy to quantify. As a result, the multiples that companies are willing to pay for those are relatively low. A credible trajectory that the buyer believes in alters that.

Essentially, people are paying a premium today for what you will do together in the future. The most significant leverage that a capable executive team has is their ability to attract further capital to overcome future challenges. This translates to a future price that is much higher than it is today. We will discuss negotiating this price in Part 2 of the book. For now, just know that the local maximum is when your future efforts dictate your price more than your current performance does.

If a buyer is interested in an acquisition in spite of the future challenges, it also shows that the buyer is committed to your mutual vision. This makes for a true long-term partner.

TEAM, BOARD, AND SHAREHOLDER ALIGNMENT

So far, we've discussed an ecosystem of strategic buyers, an understanding of the key value you bring to the table, and continued momentum in terms of performance. Prior to sitting down with your board for a formal vote, you need one more key ingredient: alignment with your board and shareholders on price and timing.

Venture-backed companies typically have investor rights that can block a sale. Investor block of a sale is no small matter. It can kill a sale and the credibility of the CEO along with it. If this happens, you can safely assume that the existing CEO will be replaced. Investors and boards have little recourse if they disagree on a sale; they have only the blunt instruments to approve the sale or go in a new strategic direction by replacing the CEO.

Knowing that the sale is going to happen with or without the current CEO's support, the most important factor to agree on is the price. Let's say that the board determines the sale price to be three times the last post-money valuation of the company. In other words, if the investors bought 10 percent of the company for $1 million, they bought the shares when the company was worth $11 million. The purchaser needs to offer $33 million or higher for that investment to be worth three times more.

It is incumbent upon the CEO to challenge their board on this point. Is everyone prepared to walk away if the offer is $32.5 million? If the answer is that the board would consider that offer, push back on the expectations. This number should not be defined as a range; the offer either exceeds the threshold, or it doesn't. Be sure to avoid confusing this number with what your company is worth—valuation is in the eye of the beholder.

Also, remember that even when you arrive at an agreed-upon number, it doesn't mean that a transaction will immediately happen if the offer is above the threshold. It just indicates that the board will evaluate an offer above that price. Avoid strong-arming a decision to reach alignment—a decision born out of tension will have painful effects later in the process.

Most investors should be thrilled with the outcome, and a handful can be neutral toward it, but none should be against the decision. This is also important in order to continue working together as a team if the acquisition falls through due to unintended consequences. Again, the most important ingredient here is trust: do the shareholders trust your judgment that this offer is the best possible outcome for everyone?

Remember that even though the decisions can be communicated verbally, always follow up in writing to materialize commitments. The rule of thumb is that no alignment is real without a paper trail so that if things don't go as expected, people can't forget the promises they've made.

Finally, make sure that this alignment is revisited with key milestones such as a signed term sheet, finalized closing documents, milestone agreements—anything and every-thing that impacts the distribution of funds needs to be communicated to maintain alignment. When it is all said and done, whether the outcome is bad, good, or great, it shouldn't be a surprise to any shareholder.

RESPONDING TO ACQUISITION
OFFERS BEFORE IT IS THE RIGHT TIME

One of the most common questions we face as mentors to other companies is about unsolicited flying offers (UFOs). What should you say if an interested party knocks on the door when you aren't ready?

David Cohen, the founder of Techstars (the largest global technology accelerator), has seen it all. Over the past fifteen years, hundreds of Techstars companies have been acquired. His first advice to founders who have a UFO in their hands is to have an honest conversation about price. Assuming that the Exit Talks have been happening, you should already have a number in your head.

The fact that there is an offer with a number should not change that figure. David counsels founders to take the floor value of any "range" that they offer for the final price. He says, "The lowest number they say is all you should hear—ignore the rest of the outreach because the actual offer is very likely to end up being very close to the low end of the range unless there are multiple competing offers. If the low number isn't high enough to be interesting, then your best bet is to simply tell them that and politely decline to provide any other information."

Understand that there is absolutely nothing more powerful you can say as a CEO than "not now" to a buyer. This is a great opportunity to kick off a discussion to create the elements of a FAIR deal and plan for an exit when the time is right. We view an acquisition offer as a great conversation starter to understand what the buyer is thinking strategically.

As a founder, you can always do that without formally evaluating an offer. For instance, a potential acquirer might get wind that you are fundraising and offer to invest in the round. Whether you let them invest or not, don't waste the opportunity to have a conversation about their rationale. Why do they see you as a good investment? An M&A team will welcome a seasoned CEO who responds maturely in the following manner: "Thank you; we are grateful to hear you are interested in investing/making an offer. We are operating according to our growth plan and believe there is still plenty of value we can capture before we can formally entertain an offer. However, I'd love to understand why you are interested in our future. Let's get to know each other."

Know that if an offer is too good to be true, it isn't true. Saying no gracefully will allow you to start building trust from a position of mutual respect, and that's a great thing. If anything, a UFO is a great checkpoint to see if you can check the boxes in our criteria. You may even see that now is the right time to sell after all.

This is also an opportunity for you to ask questions and get to better know a potential acquirer down the road. What do they care about? What do they value: tech, people, IP, top-line revenue, profitability? Remember that every interaction with a company should also be a two-way street of information flow.

CHAPTER 4

WHO ARE THE KEY STAKEHOLDERS?

N THE FAIR FRAMEWORK, ALIGNMENT IS ONE OF THE hardest elements to get right. There are so many different individuals involved on both sides of the deal.

Each side has many stakeholders, often with competing interests. And each side must be aligned internally—with the same vision, goals, and spirit of cooperation—in order to successfully get a deal done together. Add third parties like bankers and lawyers into the mix, and it can be a potent stew of egos and personalities.

As challenging as it is, make no mistake: it is the job of the startup founder to bring both teams together and ensure alignment not only on your side but on the side of your acquirers as well. There will be many aspects you cannot control, but our point here is to counsel you not to leave alignment on the buyer side to chance. Understand who all of the key decision makers are—what drives them, how they evaluate risk, and what they're looking for in the outcome.

To ensure alignment internally on both sides and create alignment when both sides come together, we first have to know who all the players are around the table.

SELL-SIDE STAKEHOLDERS

Let's begin this journey by understanding the most important players from the sell side and the roles they play in the process. Those players are:

- Key leadership of the startup
- The legal team
- The investment banker (advisor to the CEO during the sale)
- The board of directors
- The shareholders

Leadership Team
Key leadership of the startup needs to be aligned and informed during a sale. Without a concerted effort to keep

everyone on the same page and engaged in the sales conversation, you risk turning a very exciting time into one of the most miserable things you'll ever experience.

Selling a company will be one of the most distracting activities that you will take on during the entire journey of a startup. It is imperative that, as the CEO, you are being transparent with the direction you want to take the company in, as well as evaluating options around M&A when the time is right. You're also expected to do this while keeping company performance and growth moving.

The distractions will be particularly high during the evaluation period. Many acquiring companies spend this period of time asking questions and trying to understand every piece of the business. While you'll likely be part of each of these meetings, it'll be impossible to do it alone. At some point, you're going to need to rely on other members of the leadership team to help you out. If you haven't done a thorough job keeping everyone up to date with the most current information and feedback, the meetings will be much less productive—or perhaps even disastrous—without you.

Let's be honest: the very real possibility of immediate wealth creation is distracting. Experienced teams know that counting the money before the deal is done will only create problems, so they keep focused on maintaining the momentum that made the acquisition possible in the first place. Unfortunately, too many first-time founders and executive teams start creating spreadsheets to calculate their take-home proceeds modeled out at certain exit levels after just a single positive meeting early in the process. They stop prioritizing key business deliverables and start equating victory with getting the deal across the finish line.

The first problem with this is the probable consequence that a quarter (or two) of lost momentum will cause the acquirer to get cold feet. Suddenly, the projections stop looking believable, the optimism changes to doubt, and the foundations of trust begin to shake.

The second problem is the demoralization of the team if the deal falls apart for any reason.

Life is challenging at a startup. A failed deal can kill the motivation to keep pushing. If you are already fatigued from a long journey to a potential exit, being let down is a tough pill to swallow.

The important balance to strike is between transparency (to ensure leadership is aligned) and realism (to keep people focused). For most cases, we recommend the following order of communications to your leadership team:

1. Once the board formally approves an acquisition process, gather the leadership to discuss the direction. Outside of executive board members, this should be the first time they are hearing that a deal is on the horizon.

2.   Caution the team that the likely outcome is that a deal won't happen. There are a number of factors that impact the take-home price, so ask for their trust that you will represent all of their interests along with the rest of the shareholders'.

3.   Reiterate how many stars need to align for a deal to happen. Talk about the strategic nature of the potential partnership and why it makes sense to join forces. Highlight the connection to the mission to begin with—this is all that matters in the long run.

4.   Appoint one or two key executives as "advisors" to the CEO, typically the CFO and one of the key co-founders. In the early stages, this is very similar to a fundraiser. A simpler version of the financial model needs to be created along with an executive deck to tell the story of the future.

5.   Until a term sheet is signed, there should be no reason for the rest of the executive team to join the introductory meetings or the debriefs. Afterward, while the closing documents are being drawn up, they will be involved in functional diligence meetings.

6. The agreed-upon term sheet will paint the broad strokes of a transaction and should include important details like timeline, risk mitigators, and price. However, your leadership team needs to know things outside of the document—for instance, the plan to integrate, the rationale behind the transaction, and the diligence process. We recommend that the term sheet is only shared with the board and the advisor team. That being said, the signing of a term sheet calls for another alignment meeting between the key leaders in the organization.

As the certainty of closing the deal increases, the transparency around additional details such as final price, tax implications, and HR impact is critical. Remember that the more your leadership knows, the more disappointed they will be in the event of failure. Use your judgment wisely to determine when the team needs to be brought in. After all, you need them on your side for the deal to be successful once the transaction is complete.

The following page has additional thoughts on specific functions within the team and the level of transparency they need.

HIGH TRANSPARENCY

Co-Founders   Assuming that you all are significant shareholders or hold board seats, you should be up front and share everything. They are almost in your exact position and can give you the sound support that you need. This is regardless of the functional role that they hold in the company.

MID-HIGH TRANSPARENCY

Finance   Outside of your closest circle, this is the most important function to come alongside you. From various modeling needs to key questions on taxes, sales projections, revenue numbers, and runway at hand, finance needs to be right beside the CEO.

MID TRANSPARENCY

Product   Figuring out the long-term product roadmap in order to find exciting milestones to drive toward is a useful exercise. How would the products complement each other? What is the practical value for the shared customers? Your product leadership can answer these questions, but it is wasteful to have the discussion for more than one or two companies.

LOW TRANSPARENCY

Sales/   Other than customer diligence, sales and marketing teams
Marketing   should be focused all the way to ensure numbers are looking good until the signature date.

Engineering   Outside of IP review and engineering diligence calls, there really should be little need for the engineering team to interact with the M&A process.

Operations   This is the most important component. The day-to-day operations of the business, such as customer success, supply chain, HR, etc., should be kept out of the discussions until the last phase of the diligence and integration. This is typically the largest source of risk given the proximity to the customer base.

Board of Directors

A startup's board should be active. An aligned board will add credibility and support the CEO during the exit process. Founders need to articulate a clear vision to lead the strategy and execution of the deal. And investors on the board need to bring their experience to add long-term value.

In a startup, the board's main responsibility is to ask these two tough questions:

1. Do we have the right CEO?
2. Is it the right time to sell? (In other words, should we keep growing with our profits or by raising more capital?)

This is where old wounds in the fundraising process, infighting among members, and lack of ownership by the CEO during board meetings show up to hurt you. We strongly recommend following best practices in board meetings: controling the narrative, creating consistent and timely materials, and developing relevant metrics. There are excellent resources online to upgrade your performance in board meetings. Our recommendation is to add to that list an annual Exit Talk to make your life easier during the sale process of the company.

The judgment of the CEO during these discussions is a critical answer to the first responsibility of the board. By demonstrating a steady helm through these conversations, CEOs gain invaluable trust points from their boards.

Legal Team

The difference between a business lawyer and an M&A lawyer will determine not only the quality of your term sheet but also the quality of your overall exit experience. This is the only absolutely necessary component of a successful exit in terms of outside service providers. **You must—and we can't stress this enough—hire a specialist firm with experience in startup M&A.** This is not the time to hire your friendly startup lawyer who has never done a transaction before. Do not feel an obligation to the team that has supported you during the fundraising process or day-to-day legal support. If they have your best interest at heart, they will likely recommend a colleague who specializes in startup M&A.

An unsophisticated legal team will lead to subpar understanding of deal risks, or worse, unwarranted paranoia about every term proposed by the opposing counsel. A good lawyer will identify the most important points to negotiate and will not create unnecessary obstacles. "What you want to make sure you do," said David Sobota, who leads corp dev at Instacart after thirteen years at Google, "is assess how goal-oriented and pragmatic your legal team is. Make sure they know the job is to get over the finish line and not get bogged down in minutiae."

Furthermore, from complicated tax matters to measuring exposure in the escrow terms, there are too many factors that require specialization and experience to go with, say, your cousin from Columbus. Even the best of relationships won't make up for the price you'll pay for lack of expertise. You never want to realize that the reason you got screwed on a deal was because your lawyer made a mistake.

Use the best legal team you can afford, and work with your board and shareholders to get recommendations on firms. This will lead to an efficient process, and you will have sound judgment on your side throughout the process.

Investment Bankers
While there is a clear reason that bankers exist, it is unclear if every startup acquisition needs one. In the event a banker is necessary, it's important for first-time founders (and all founders, for that matter) to know how to conduct diligence before hiring a banker and the best ways to utilize one.

A credible investment banker who has worked with the acquirer in the past can help accelerate the process. A banker also signals that there are multiple potential buyers involved. But this is a dicey game that does not always work out in your favor. All in all, a banker polishes the company before an acquisition through coaching, broad outreach, or strategic relationship building.

In an ideal world, they help you negotiate better terms for the deal by creating competition around it. If this were all bankers added to the equation, it would make total sense to include them in every sale. Unfortunately, it is not always an ideal world, and sometimes they add more headaches (and costs) than they're worth.

There are two components to a banker's fee:

- A monthly escrow that will count toward the final fees. This can be negotiated down to zero in most cases, accompanied by the proper percentage fee.

- A percentage of the final acquisition price. It is crucial to confirm how the payment will take place in various scenarios. Will the payment come out before or after the escrow is taken out? What if there are milestone payments tied to the deal? Make sure the bankers are aligned on the structure you want in the deal. We have seen numbers ranging from 1 to 5 percent for average-sized deals in the technology space.

A good rule of thumb is to remember that most tech deals for under $75 million (as of 2021) are typically done without bankers. In those cases, the CEO uses their existing network to find a buyer and negotiate a fair price for the right exit. For these types of tech acquisitions, founders should be doing the work to identify interested parties and build relationships in their buyer ecosystem. This is not an absolute rule, just a suggestion to proceed with care.

That being said, there are legendary examples of bankers creating immense value—for instance, the famous role that Mike Grimes from Morgan Stanley played in the WhatsApp transaction. In February 2014, a report he authored leaked to the senior executive offices of Google, Facebook, and many other notable tech companies. It essentially analyzed the same growth data that Sequoia and Facebook used to identify WhatsApp as a key acquisition target.

Years later, the sector still buzzes with speculation as to what exactly happened. Did Mike leak the information on purpose to make the market more competitive? Was this an honest mistake? We can't be sure. We do know that report ultimately led to an initial meeting between Jan Koum and Larry Page, then-CEO of Google. While the meeting with Google wasn't successful (Page was half an hour late), it set off the frenzied pace of events that led Mark Zuckerberg to offer an essentially blank check, and the largest technology acquisition in modern history closed for $19 billion.

The banker who represented WhatsApp in the deal? Mike Grimes from Morgan Stanley.

If you decide to hire a banker, obviously hiring the right one is critical, and you should undertake a thorough diligence period to determine the right fit. Evaluate everything from personal chemistry to relevant network access in your target industry. A banker is essentially a broker, and you can save a lot of time by paying for experience.

Once you like a team, confirm that the partner on the deal will be present in the conversations. Request a list of past CEOs they have worked with, and evaluate past transactions they have been involved in. Avoid people who claim that they have a 100 percent close rate on the deals they decide to facilitate—this is virtually impossible.

Shareholders

With all other elements in place, there's still one final piece to your exit that needs to be strategically managed and accounted for. The majority of preferred shareholders will need to approve the final transaction. Without their approval, you have no way to move forward.

You will likely need consent from the majority of shareholders for both common and preferred shares. Typically, the common shares are mostly made up of the founding team, so assuming that you are aligned internally, that should be the easier part.

Your preferred shareholders will also have to give you their blessing. They all need to agree with you, and with each other, that this is the right time to sell. You must have the majority on your side—there is no other way to force the hand of an unwilling investor without things getting ugly.

And you want to make sure things don't get ugly with investors right before an exit because corp dev teams avoid these situations like the plague. Even with an escrow set aside to mitigate future problems, no one wants to deal with the fallout from angry investors down the road.

Your best-case scenario is that you have support from the start—that all shareholders trust your judgment through effective board management and company leadership. Clear, transparent investor updates will make sure that your investors are already familiar with the key challenges, opportunities, and timeline ahead. It will build the trust you need to move forward with their support.

We also recommend that you provide transparent communication even after the board shows their support. The assumption here is that you have an active board that includes your largest shareholders. Having a near-majority included on your side in your initial outreach makes it easier for the shareholders to feel good about the upcoming deal. When in doubt, overcommunicate. Make yourself available for one-on-one phone calls. Explain why the timing is FAIR, and confirm that there is certainty to close. Use all the trust you have accumulated to win your investors over and cross the finish line.

And get them over the finish line you must because one of the critical components of the closing docs is the **consent threshold**—the percentage of approving shareholders you need in order to execute the transaction. Keep open lines of communication, and make sure to use a digital signature tool similar to DocuSign at all costs. Depending on the risk tolerance of the buyer, the threshold can range from 51 percent to 100 percent! The rule of thumb is that the simpler the cap table (i.e., the fewer investors to manage), the easier your life is going to be.

So far, we've covered all of the key stakeholders on the startup side of the table. Next, we evaluate the buyer side of the equation.

BUY-SIDE STAKEHOLDERS

Now that we know all the key players from your side of the acquisition, it's important to know who you'll be talking to and negotiating with throughout the process on the buyer's side. Although these aren't hard rules, you can expect to talk to a representative from each of these groups during any sale. Here's who you need to be aware of:

- The corporate development team acts as the air traffic control throughout the process.
- The business unit is the ultimate home for the startup within the parent.
- Executive leadership negotiates the final terms of the purchase.
- Buyer legal teams need to be managed throughout the process.
- There are unique cases where buyers have their own bankers.

- Final approvals come from the board of directors.
- With big enough mergers, large public shareholders need to approve, along with the US government through the Federal Trade Commission.

Once there is stable, continuous alignment internally, it is imperative to ensure the same happens on the buy side. As the CEO, you are in a unique position. You'll be negotiating a complex process, often with opposing opinions and goals, with individuals you'll need to collaborate with immediately after the deal is done. With this in mind, approach every conversation, especially the tough ones, with empathy, collaboration, and confidence in mind. You're going to need it.

It is almost guaranteed that not everything will go according to plan. Tensions may rise. Conflict is inevitable, and maintaining alignment is difficult. In order to achieve the best outcome possible, you need to know who all of the other players are on the other side and their own processes for achieving alignment. Let's begin with the air traffic control of the process: the corporate development team.

Corporate Development Team

There are many names for the core group of executives who are responsible for buying companies: M&A team, corporate development, business development. Consider this group the quarterback of the entire operation. They are the ones herding each side to a final decision. In certain companies, M&A teams operate as an extension of the product development team—for instance, at Apple. While the leadership makes the final call, Apple views M&A as a key part of developing new products, with notable examples like NeXT, Siri, iPod, and many others.

In other companies, M&A is much more focused on long-term business strategy than on product. This is one of the first questions that an entrepreneur should ask when they meet a new company: what is the strategic objective of their acquisition engine? Before you can move forward in any exit process, you need to be able to understand—but more importantly, agree with—their overall strategic vision and the steps they've identified that will help get them to their goals.

The Business Unit

Next, you will evaluate the business unit on the buyer's side. This will be the ultimate home for your startup within the parent company when the deal is done. It is your final destination and thus, it is imperative to develop relationships with as many people as possible in this group throughout the process. There will be times that the acquiring company will close these doors until a deal is complete, so do as much work as you can as early as possible so that you have all the necessary information to make the right exit for you and your company.

If you get the sense that the buyers closed the doors to their business unit too soon or too frequently, it might indicate that the buyer has an opaque culture with siloed operations or doubts that the deal will get across the finish line. This is a point to lean forward and make these connections happen.

Ask about who you will be reporting to, as this is the clearest signal toward your ultimate home. After the first meeting with that stakeholder, you need to be able to clearly articulate their goals and objectives with your acquisition. This is extremely critical because their goals and objectives will ultimately come to define the integration process. Sometimes you fall in love with the person they are recommending that you report to. Sometimes the chemistry is just not there. Don't panic. Take more time to get to know that person. If the fit is just not there, there is an opportunity to go to the deal lead from corp dev (or the CEO, if you are dealing with them directly) and gently and respectfully ask for alternatives or suggestions. If there are no alternatives, this actually might be a deal-killer. Most mergers don't pan out when the CEO and their new direct report don't see eye to eye. As we all know, a bad boss can suck the joy out of life.

Just like any relationship within the acquirer, these relationships are best built over time to understand complementary businesses. Remember that the best rationale isn't to join forces with a competitor; it is unlocking new levels of growth for both companies.

Having an ally parallel to the corporate development team is key to push for better terms. If the business unit is product-oriented, inquire about the key metrics your technology will impact. Use these conversations to define the internal value of your startup. This is the best leverage in the long term; a clearly articulated vision will soften terms to your advantage.

Depending on the place in the organizational structure, this leader is typically different from the group who will need to sign off on the purchase.

Executive Leadership

On the buy side, the top executive (usually the CEO) is the final approver of the terms of the purchase. This is where the buck stops in the organization. Typically, the corporate development team reports directly to the CEO or the CFO. For any meaningful transaction, both these groups will need to give their blessing.

This is, bar none, the best entry into the process. A relationship built over a long time with a seasoned CEO will give the most tangible insights into rationale, defining complementary avenues and ensuring the smoothest process.

Even for a company worth above $1 trillion like Amazon, this is no exception. To date, Jeff Bezos personally signs off on every deal worth above $10 million.

This is also the final thread to pull during the negotiation process. If the deal terms are at an impasse, this is the only person who can make a difference.

There is no better way that we can demonstrate the importance of a healthy, proactive relationship with executive leadership than Mark's personal encounter with Bill Gates. After the Whitewater Group sold to Symantec, Mark ran a small company of game developers called Kinesoft. One day, a genius programmer on the team figured out how to move the bits around the screen fast enough to play Sega and Nintendo scrolling action arcade games on personal computers for the very first time.

This revolutionary breakthrough at Kinesoft happened to line up as Microsoft was planning their own game-changing software with the launch of Windows 95. After years of trying, Windows 95 was finally ready to take on Macintosh as the operating system for everyone.

Kinesoft moved quickly to reframe their business model by creating a porting engine that would take existing Sega and Nintendo games and easily bring them over and convert them to Windows 95. In essence, Kinesoft became the bridge between the multibillion-dollar console gaming market and the emerging multibillion-dollar PC market.

Mark quickly signed deals with major game publishers to port their titles over to Windows 95 in anticipation of its launch in April 1995. This started to get the attention of the major industry players, and by March 1995, Sega, Intel, and IBM all tried to either invest in or buy Kinesoft.

All of this culminated one Monday afternoon with a phone call from Microsoft. It was one of Bill's lieutenants, reaching out to Mark for help:

"Bill Gates is at Spring Comdex in Atlanta, and he has a problem. Tomorrow morning, he is scheduled to give the keynote address where he is officially going to introduce and launch Windows 95. His presentation is going to show Windows at work and Windows at home, where he is going to show a game that Microsoft developed for Windows 95. Except our game doesn't work. Can you fly to Atlanta tonight and show your game that runs on Windows 95 to him?"

Mark immediately hopped on a plane to Atlanta. He arrived at Bill's suite around midnight and demonstrated the Kinesoft team's work. The next day in his presentation, Bill not only launched Windows 95, but he also gave a demo of the very game Mark had shown him just hours earlier. Bill even called Kinesoft out and gave them credit in front of the world. Unbeknownst to Mark, he also met with Masayoshi Son, the CEO of SoftBank, who had just bought Comdex, and they decided to form a new joint venture game company to create games for Windows.

Weeks later, IBM came in with an offer to buy the company. IBM was launching their new operating system called OS2, and they wanted Kinesoft to help build their games studio.

After some fevered negotiations, Mark verbally agreed to all the major deal points and headed to LA for the very first E3 games show. The goal was to make a major joint announcement. Meanwhile, while the attorneys headed to New York with the signed deal documents. It looked like everything was in order.

Mark arrived in LA on a Monday. The big announcement and press conference was scheduled for Thursday. However, back in New York, the IBM attorneys started changing the deal. Nothing was bad enough to kill the deal entirely, but it was onerous enough to give the young founder pause. Big company lawyers twisting the knife at the last minute to "protect" their clients.

Within the same hour, Mark also got a call from Japan. It was an immediate meeting request from Masayoshi Son. Mark patiently explained that he couldn't fly to Japan, that Kinesoft was about to announce a deal with IBM. Masa would not take no for an answer: "We promise we will make this worth your while. Bill Gates said we *have* to work with you!"

The next morning the two partners were ushered into a meeting with Masayoshi Son while the attorneys in New York were at an impasse.

After the usual pleasantries, Masa looked at both of them and asked, "How much for your company? Bill Gates says you are the only company in the world that can build Windows games at scale." Not bad for an introduction!

Mark didn't blink. He gave a number that was four times what IBM was offering them. Masa accepted on the spot. They shook hands, and eleven days later, the deal was closed and the money was in the bank.

This kind of speed is only possible if you are working with the ultimate decision-makers.

Legal Teams

Buyers will have their own legal representation as outside counsel. They usually consist of a key group of stakeholders that you hopefully never directly interact with. It is safe to assume that the buyer will use sophisticated counsel with plenty of experience in acquiring companies.

The most important point to keep in mind is that you should never negotiate directly with lawyers. Keep the back-and-forth to a minimum while working out the issues, and always go through your own (highly experienced!) counsel. If there are strategic decisions that need to be made, they should be decided between business unit members or executive leaders, not between the two legal teams. These guidelines will help ensure that you don't get bogged down in legal minutiae or spin cycles (and billable hours) arguing the wrong point with the wrong person.

Investment Bankers/Advisors

There are unique cases where buyers will have their own bankers or a group of third-party advisors for the sale. While these are rare, they will typically show up in cross-industry deals—such as a manufacturing company purchasing a software company.

Board of Directors

This is the hardest group of stakeholders to penetrate and the group with the highest degree of power. Regardless of the approval of the executive stakeholders, the business unit, and the corporate development team, the board of directors will need to formally approve the transaction to continue.

More often than not, this is a rubber stamp. The buyer stakeholder group will need to socialize the deal before it is formally up for a vote to ensure success. It is unrealistic to expect you will have access to this sacred chamber of influence in the company.

Large companies are protective of their board discussions. These are closed-door meetings and have formal functions other than advising the CEO. Just like a healthy board in a startup, directors do not directly manage the business of the company, but they are ultimately responsible for the management of the corporation. They have the ultimate attention of the CEO, as they have the power to remove that person from their role.

Most large companies disclose their board members on their website. This is a relationship-building effort over a long period of time. The best board members will give visibility to the strategic direction of the company, which, in turn, allows you to build a strong rationale.

This might sound outlandish, but never underestimate the power you have as an up-and-coming startup in an industry. Seasoned board members appreciate your insights as a fresh perspective. Of course, you can learn from their experience over time, but the relationship is mutually beneficial. Moreover, intentional relationships with board members give you access to extremely warm introductions to the right business unit, executive leader, or corporate development team when the timing is right.

Remember that this is a way to kick-start discussions. A board member is not going to be making the executive decision to buy your company. Once the formal process begins, avoid stepping outside your relationships to ensure they are aligned on the direction. No board member can save a damaged relationship with a CEO.

With big enough mergers, large public shareholders will need to approve the deals, along with the US government through the Federal Trade Commission. The Hart-Scott-Rodino (HSR) Act requires that parties to certain transactions—including mergers and acquisitions, acquisitions of voting securities, and assets and minority investments—file notifications with the Department of Justice Antitrust Division and the Federal Trade Commission; they must also observe a statutory waiting period if the transaction meets specified size-of-person and size-of-transaction thresholds. This dollar amount is referred to as the HSR threshold, and as of March 2021, the figure is $92 million. If your deal is worth more than that, you will have some additional paperwork to file.[7]

In 2021, mega-acquisitions like Plaid by Visa were being called off due to antitrust concerns. Facebook received a federal probe into its Instagram acquisition. Big Tech is under scrutiny, just like Microsoft was in the nineties, for being too powerful.

These deals are well into billions, and both sides understand that once they come to terms, this still doesn't mean a deal is going to happen. It's also true that much reform is needed in the evaluation process of these acquisitions. Antitrust laws were not created for modern companies like Instagram and Facebook.

In 2019, Mark Zuckerberg defended the Instagram purchase, and again in 2020, by attributing the mega-success of the acquisition to the unique resources Facebook gave to the smaller company. He further boasted that this purchase was reviewed and approved by state regulators at the time.

Sarah Friar wrote in *No Filter*,[8] an excellent book about the story of Instagram's journey, about how the process was evaluated. When Facebook went public, the FTC kicked off an investigation to first answer a simple question: were Facebook and Instagram competing with each other? At the time,

Facebook had just started its advertising business model, and Instagram did not have a business model to begin with.

The process began with the FTC inquiring what Facebook thought of Instagram and vice versa. However, this documentation was not collected by investigators. The lawyers who worked on making the deal happen were now tasked with finding evidence against the deal. The companies paid them to investigate themselves.

The firms did a thorough job and found documents that hinted at competition. However, the same lawyers pointed out that Facebook lived in a tough world; its very own camera app had far fewer users than Instagram. They pointed out plenty of companies with millions of users in the photo-sharing-app world such as Path and PicPlz. They painted a picture that showed Facebook was not the dominant force gobbling up smaller companies; it was the underdog in the market.

The regulators did not understand the winner-take-all model of these internet businesses. Instagram had thirty million users at the time of the acquisition. By the end of that summer, it had nearly doubled. While the application looked like anyone could copy it, the real value was the massive size of the content library compared to new entrants.

The FTC investigation that summer happened behind closed doors, with no public report of its findings. Facebook highlighted that the process was robust, and when it was all over, the regulators indicated that no further action was needed.

The evolution of the regulatory landscape will be fascinating to follow in the upcoming years. It is likely that the current Wild West will lend itself to a similar scrutiny in industries such as oil, construction, and media.

Similarly, the stakeholders that approve a FAIR exit agreement will evolve as more deals are made with different kinds of companies. While this may change the conversations you have, both in content and frequency, there are a few truths that will remain. You need to be as transparent and proactive as possible. As the founder, it's your responsibility to ensure everyone feels comfortable and informed. Not only is it best practice, but these habits could mean the difference of millions of dollars in your bank account.

CHAPTER 5

WHAT DOES CORPORATE DEVELOPMENT WANT YOU TO KNOW?

URING THE RESEARCH PHASE OF THIS BOOK, WE met many executives from some of the largest technology companies today: Twitter, Amazon, Facebook, Pinterest, Atlassian, and many others. Gary Johnson stood out as the person who has seen it all.

Gary's journey with corporate development began at Apple in the early 2000s. While he worked as a software manager, he came to understand the power of acquisitions and the role they played in every major product launch. In a series of interviews, he reflected, "Without acquiring companies and their technologies, there is no way Apple could have developed all of the in-house technical capacity to launch any of the game-changing products of the twenty-first century."

After Apple, he spent a few years in the finance world advising both private and public companies and then signed on to head the acquisition team at Facebook. There he was involved in major deals from the time of Instagram through Oculus, until he left to join Pinterest's executive team as the new Global Head of Corporate and Business Development.

Gary was the first person to introduce us to his key elements of Alignment, Integration and Rationale (our humble suggestion was to add Fit!). To him, corporate development is like conducting an orchestra. He identifies the key opportunities, ensures that there is continuous alignment within the organization, and takes the time to make the founders feel at home in their new destination.

He believes that the most important component of successful corporate development is to understand that the real work begins once the deal closes. As long as the objective is sound and the teams trust each other, he doesn't let small issues escalate into major conflict.

Most importantly, he designs integration with the founders in the center of the process. A good corporate development executive builds long-term relationships and becomes an expert in the companies on the technology horizon.

He sat with us for a series of interviews for this book. His candor and wisdom are the backbone of the following chapter as he expounded on the question, "What do you wish entrepreneurs knew about M&A before they met you?"

What we want to stress is that the executives who will be spearheading and guiding the deal on the other side are not working against you. And they are not the enemy. Rather, they are simply looking to augment the value of the companies they represent and want to do that with the most talented, trustworthy entrepreneurs they can find. At best, they will be your ambassador and guide throughout the journey. At worst, they will kill transactions to protect the parent.

Gary has done over $30 billion worth of deals, and he would be the first to tell you M&A is the lifeblood of Silicon Valley. The big players need you. And you have more power than you think. Don't expect perfect transparency from the other side, and there are many parts of the process you are not in control of. However, there are some things you can do to make your life and your counterpart's life easier.

BOTH PARTIES NEED TO LEAVE BAGGAGE FROM PAST TRANSACTIONS BEHIND

There's no getting around it: starting a serious dialogue with the corporate development team of a potential acquirer can be fraught with uncertainty and doubt.

The questions that swirl in founders' brains are intense and overwhelming: *What are they thinking on the other side of the negotiating table? What are their goals? Are they trying to take advantage of me? Do they know I'm nervous? Will this be similar to my past trauma with our first attempt at getting acquired?*

But you have to check those impulses, assume good intentions, and, most importantly, leave the baggage from past transactions at the door.

Founders shouldn't bring their prior relationship experience to the beginning of the new one. If founders were burned and mistreated in other transactions, close the book on those folks and move on. As a founder, you are in the pattern recognition business, so we understand how hard it may be to move on from negative experiences in the past, but it is critical to your future success.

Chalk it up to a lack of FAIR elements in the last transaction and move on. If anything, resilience will be a refreshing perspective for the buyers to see in you. They do many more deals than you do and find it much easier to leave behind any negative experiences. When they can recognize that same attitude in you, they will feel an inherent level of trust that you can lead, even through tough times.

The truth is founders, like all people, crave certainty—and an exit is a very uncertain process. Not only are you terrified of making wrong decisions for a company you've dedicated your life to, but you're also worried about money, leadership, and all the changes that come from a merger or acquisition. Corporate development executives understand how you're feeling; they've seen it a million times.

Good corporate development executives will allow you to navigate these tensions without any judgment. However, as an act of good faith, and because it's what's best for your own well-being, do what you can to let go of any negative feelings born from past events. Approach each new conversation as if it's your first one.

EXPAND YOUR CONTACT LIST

While your corporate development leader is most often your main contact and point of communication, you should not rely solely on them to be your champion. Your job is to establish relationships—with the blessing and partnership of your corporate development leader—with as many people throughout the acquiring company as appropriate.

You will need to gather important data about their business, build a network of support to polish your rationale and build alignment, and start to understand and mutually build an integration plan.

Hilary Shirazi was a corp dev leader at LinkedIn and Zendesk before joining Pinterest as Head of Corporate Development. Over a series of interviews, she gave us amazing access to her view on M&A from the acquirers' side of the table. One thing she emphasized was the importance of expanding your network internally outside of your main point of contact. "There's no question that the more people who know you and vouch for you inside the organization, the better," she said. "When we are making our case and there are more heads nodding in recognition among our internal stakeholders, that helps to grease the wheels."

UNDERSTANDING THE DILIGENCE PROCESS: WHAT TO EXPECT

The goal of diligence is basically to answer three questions. The first covers the product, tech, or data you're offering—your key asset. Simply put, they want to know if the IP is really yours. Next, they want to look at the people you're leading. Can your team reach the goals the acquirer has for their future? The answer here will determine the long-term success of the potential deal. Finally, executives need to trust that your customers will stick around. They are only interested in revenue they can predict will grow in the immediate and long-term future.

The diligence process for IP will likely begin with checking your employee agreements for all staff and contractors to ensure ownership. They will also evaluate your code to check proprietary and open sources in case of potential IP infringement or cybersecurity flaws. Remember, larger companies are open to significantly more legal risk than the small startup, and any hint of a possible lawsuit can freeze a deal in its tracks.

Diligence for your team will involve buyer representatives from product and corporate development teams sitting down with the engineers and other identified key individuals. They are looking to get a read on the cultural fit between the two parties, along with validating their strategic assumptions. Understanding this can be a highly anxious process, founders typically believe this is where the big company is coming to get their "secret sauce." Trust us. The last thing an M&A team wants is to be accused of stealing! Remember that they are looking for hints in general culture fit and alignment on the future vision from the team in parallel. Hilary Shirazi took pains to dispel this fear in our interview: "There is a misconception that the big company is just going to change their whole trajectory and steal your thing. But corporations are well-oiled machines with long-term horizon planning. This really shouldn't keep founders up at night."

Sarah Hughes, the Director of Corporate Development at Atlassian, echoed Hilary's views. This was her first response when asked, "What do you wish more founders knew?" She said, "CEOs have been trained, mostly by VCs, to not share. I want people to know that with very few exceptions (like specific tech IP), what corp dev is asking for does not constitute trade secrets. It doesn't serve you to hide information. Big companies generally don't steal stuff like crazy weirdos. They aren't going to take that info and do anything. They have long-term plans and agendas that take a lot more energy and effort to steer in different directions."

As for the investigation into your customers, try not to worry too much about this. Remember that the bigger company likely has many, many more customers than you do. The goal of this diligence is not to take them away. They want to validate that the product you created is solving a real problem for them. Depending on the number of customers, diligence will look different, but they all have the same goal in mind: they want to ensure long-term success for themselves and for you and your team.

As with everything else in this book, it's best to prepare for the diligence process as soon as possible. An organized due diligence process is the result of a highly organized team. A messy diligence process can kill deals. We've seen it happen. The best approach is to stay prepared from the beginning. Keep your house clean from day one so that you're not overwhelmed or surprised in the critical diligence process.

"Entrepreneurs need to run a tight ship," said Chris Hecht, Head of Corporate Development at Atlassian. "We've stopped deals when the data room was incomplete."

A sloppy and incomplete data room can make you look unprofessional, slow down the transaction to a crawl, and rack up expensive lawyer fees as they chase down documents. It can give key employees potential leverage over you at the last minute, and it signals to the acquirer that you either have a weak management team or are not serious about the deal.

Needless to say, you should have this ready before the process begins instead of scrambling at the last minute.

An introductory data room should include:

Financials	All up-to-date financial reports including audited statements and future projections.
Intellectual Property	A product deck, overview of IP, and any issued patents should be enough. Also be sure to include any prior patent or trademark infringement claims from outside parties (and how they were resolved). Nothing will kill a deal faster than a fuzzy view of who owns what.
HR	Make sure that all employees have signed employee agreements with IP assignments to the company, including all patent and trademark filings, and make sure that all outside contractors have signed clear waivers of IP ownership. Clear documentation of payroll should reflect no unusual payment setups for old employees or immigration issues.
Legal	The full and complete history of all corporate documentation, legal agreements, and board minutes. If there are past issues that you dealt with, they need to be articulated clearly.

HOW AND WHY TO ASK THE RIGHT QUESTIONS

Of course, as with investors, due diligence is a two-way street. Corporate development professionals expect you to ask questions of them with the same vigor as they investigate your company. Asking questions makes a CEO appear more sophisticated and more worthy of acquisition. Again, Hilary Shirazi provides excellent insight: "The harder the questions founders ask me, the more I know they are serious."

Further, larger companies have you at a disadvantage due to experience with greater volumes of transactions and the inherent information asymmetry that exists in the process. Your job, at all times, is to know as much as you possibly can about the acquiring company, their strategic objectives, their decision-making process, who the key players are, and what they care about. It is a daunting task.

Dave Sobota, Head of Corporate Development at Instacart, encourages entrepreneurs to be proactive in asking questions. The more questions you ask and the more you understand, the easier it will be to work in partnership with the acquiring company to help them craft and justify the right purchasing rationale to buy your company. You should be taking an active hand in shaping your own destiny. He implores entrepreneurs, "If corp dev isn't explaining their reasoning or process to you, you have to stop them and ask, 'Who is excited? Should I get a banker? What happens next?'"

Some good examples of questions to ask that corporate development should be happy to answer:

- What is your rationale for wanting to buy our company?
- What is the strategic hole you need to plug?

- Are you feeling pressure from a competitor who is already addressing this problem?
- Are your customers asking for this solution?
- Which division will we reside in once we are acquired?
- Who will be our new boss? Are they involved with this process? If not, why not?
- How will you measure success post-transaction, and what kind of budget/resources will we have to execute?
- What is the decision-making process? Who has to approve?

The answers to these questions will be obvious if the process is FAIR. You are essentially drawing the outline of what is going to be in the term sheet. For instance, if you don't like the price tag in the term sheet, point to the rationale and the strategic value instead of complaining. Remember that your startup is like a koi fish; it will grow to the size of the tank it is put in. Understanding future resources gives you powerful hints about how much you are really worth.

Answers to questions can be found in lots of places. The place to start is with corp dev, but savvy entrepreneurs won't stop there. In many tech companies, for example, the product manager often has the final say. It is really important to get to know them, and by doing so, you will make corporate development's life easier.

Who are the influencers? What do the industry analysts think? What about the stock analysts? If the acquiring company is a public company, information around strategic priorities can be found by listening in on the public earnings calls or reading their transcripts. With LinkedIn, it's pretty easy to track down former executives of a company, and you may be surprised what you will discover by reaching out to them. And of course, don't forget to talk to the CEOs of companies that the acquiring company has bought in the past.

Remember, knowledge is power. You can't outsource this. It's your job to be seeking this out on an ongoing basis.

SUCCESS MEANS THAT THE DEAL IS FAIR FOR ALL PARTIES

Corporate development executives are graded on the relative smoothness of the acquisition process and your subsequent success at the parent company. This is where their interests and incentives lie. The best among them are able to chaperone the future into existence with their judgment—and they are rewarded handsomely for it.

Gary Johnson took pains to stress that M&A is a grounded, sober activity. It's not about "bright shiny objects." They are always looking for Fit, Alignment, Integration, and Rationale—this makes the job complex and difficult. Your job is to work with your corp dev counterpart to help them craft and perfect their FAIR story.

Trust is the currency that makes it work.

As we discussed earlier, trust is the lifeblood of M&A. It takes time to build and has to be earned with each and every interaction. And it can be squandered in an instant with the perception of a lie or a misleading or exaggerated statement. Never lie. Ever. Never make a claim that you can't back up. In the end they will find out, and it will always come back to bite you.

Corporate development executives want you to know that there are bad players out there. In the past, a company that was known for bad practices was Microsoft in the nineties— luring companies in with the prospects of an acquisition only to walk away at the last second. Acquisition was used as a weapon to take out competitors, and there are still companies that behave this way today.

However, until proven otherwise, you are better off assuming good intent. The reality is that most companies with bad reputations have them for a reason, and a wise founder will have the relationships in place to do back-channel checks. Truly nasty behavior typically shows up in articles in the tech industry, and the responsibility is on you to identify the bad partners.

This is the real value of trust built over the long term. More often than not, bad actors behave in those ways in a consistent manner. Life is too short to do business with assholes, and we recommend you stay away from those folks no matter what the payout might look like.

Because trust is so important, corporate development will understand if you want to keep the cards close to your chest in certain parts of the process. Especially as the companies are getting to know each other, it's perfectly acceptable to say, "We're going to pass on answering that for now, and here's why." This kind of communication builds trust and leads both parties to a FAIR exit that is right for everyone. Certain parts of your business will include trade secrets and IP that you should protect at all costs. But don't confuse protecting your core IP with sharing the details the prospective buyer needs to get the deal done.

Remember that most due diligence is to confirm what the buyer is assuming. Unless there is a reason for broken trust, corporate development will push for diligence to be completed in a timely manner. They will have much more leverage internally to push for urgency than you will, so invest as much trust as possible.

As Stefan Williams, Head of Corporate Development at Snowflake, told us, founders should "extend their vision past what is possible today and imagine a future with the resources and leverage that a much larger company can bring." Remember that the acquisition is ultimately about the future, supported by the credibility of your past actions.

PART 2

NEGOTIATING THE RIGHT EXIT

Now that you've identified the correct fit for your company, ensured alignment, and understood and agreed to the rationale, it's time to get into the thick of it. Before you can focus on successful integration, you have to master the negotiation. Here is where you'll be able to see if you've planned the right exit for you and your team or if you need to find a more FAIR partnership.

During this time, remember that negotiation begins way before an offer is made, and everything is up for negotiation.

From carve-outs, escrows, earn-outs, compensation packages, post-acquisition resources, and, of course, the big brass-knuckle ring of purchase price, there are seemingly endless terms to negotiate. It's intense and overwhelming. The cauldron of stress is always threatening to boil over as founders find themselves on unfamiliar new terrain.

This is also the phase where more people come to the party—where bankers and lawyers can swoop in to add or subtract value.

If you are lucky enough to entertain an offer for your startup, the chances are the negotiation phase is where the deal will fall apart. That's the bad news.

But since when have odds ever held an entrepreneur back?

"It's so damn exciting when someone says they want to buy your company," said Cliff Shaw, calling from his farmhouse in the south of France, where he now lives with his wife and daughter after successfully selling his startup Mocavo a few years ago. Cliff chalks up his last success to the fact that on his first two attempts, he made nearly every negotiation mistake in the book. He dedicated himself to learning from those mistakes and now regularly mentors other founders on how to navigate the exit. He shared his wisdom over the course of several Chicago-to-Provence chats.

His advice, as well as our own stories, inform this next section.

As we make our way through this messy middle phase, we will break down the elements of a term sheet, the closing documents, and all of the variables and terminology founders need to know. We'll talk about the best way to manage a legal team and how to work well with your bankers. But before we dive deep into the technical terms and the cast of characters, we first want to take a high-level view to explore some general principles and best practices.

Maybe you're a seasoned negotiator, or maybe you're just a beginner. But even if you count yourself in the ranks of the former, it's likely that you haven't sold more than a few companies before. And selling your company is a whole different ballgame. You will likely be dealing with M&A professionals on the other side of the table who conduct dozens of transactions every year.

There's no way around it: the odds are against you. The first rule that applies across the board is that the acquirer has done this more than you have. You are up against a team of executives who make a living doing deals like yours. There are rare moments of leverage in this negotiation you are about to enter, and our goal is to identify those points.

This phase of an M&A transaction is an intense period of negotiation not only for price but for the future of your company, your team, and your relationships.

Inexperienced founders may feel like they've lost the fight even before things kick off. But it's crucial to adjust that mindset. Seasoned founders replace the "us versus them" mentality with one that treats acquirers as future partners and colleagues.

So how do you go up against a better-funded, more sophisticated future partner? How do you navigate successfully so that the result of the transaction is that the buyer is stronger and more valuable than they were before? How do you make sure your own team is aligned and protected? We'll tell you.

CHAPTER 6

WHERE DO VALUATIONS COME FROM?

W HEN FACEBOOK BOUGHT INSTAGRAM IN 2012 for a cool $1 billion, it was the WTF heard around the startup world. Heads jerked up from Bloomberg terminals. Analysts exchanged knowing looks, and "Zuckerberg finally blew it" emails landed in inboxes from Silicon Valley to Hong Kong.

Business and tech journalists were flummoxed. At the time, Instagram had just thirty million users, thirteen employees, and $0 of revenue. Almost $1 billion in exchange for $0 of revenue seemed like an odd trade, to say the least. Admittedly an outlier—most acquired tech startups see price tags that are nowhere near this vicinity—the acquisition highlights a key principle of startup M&A.

The purchase price of a tech startup can be influenced by the invested dollars, previous valuations of the company, lifetime value of each customer, credible growth rates, etc. However, the only true price of a technology company is what an acquirer is willing to pay for it.

When members of the C-suite of an interested acquirer come knocking on your door, they already have an invest-ment thesis about what your company is going to do for them; they are already oriented to future value. If you are looking at buyers to proactively sell to, you have to make the case for what that future value is. But either way, if you are going to earn the maximum amount off of any deal, future value is where it comes from. That doesn't mean the past isn't important. Of course, you need growth and a history of past performance that demonstrates value and credibility toward your future plans.

However, the most important part of a buyer's deci-sion-making process for the price they are willing to pay comes down to the potential future value of the acquired company within the larger corporation.

UNDERSTAND HOW THE ACQUIRING COMPANY THINKS ABOUT FUTURE VALUE, AND LEARN AS MUCH AS YOU CAN

You need to be aware of how different roles within a larger company will view the potential acquisition in order to successfully position your company as valuable to the buyers. While some (like CTOs and CFOs) will often look only at the past performance of your company, highlighting the potential risks, it doesn't mean that the deal is impossible. If the CEO and sales leaders see something in your company that aligns with their vision for the future, it's your responsibility to help the others see that too. Understand the terrain and play the game. CTO and CFO objections can be overcome, but you have to understand the acquiring company's business case inside and out.

At the time of the Instagram acquisition, most experts derided Zuckerberg as inexperienced and foolhardy. With his company on the verge of an IPO, he pulled valuable resources to spend on what, at face value, was a nascent social network that didn't make any money.

So what did Zuckerberg see? Why was he so intent on getting the deal done (his second attempt) that he personally negotiated the terms with Instagram founder Kevin Systrom while the legal teams waited and watched TV together? In short, he saw the future.

Since its acquisition in 2012, Instagram's user base has grown to more than a billion users and today accounts for a quarter of Facebook's ad revenues: $20 billion a year as of 2019. To put this in perspective, in the same year, YouTube brought in just over $15 billion. Today, Instagram's value is estimated at over $100 billion—it makes up a huge chunk of Facebook. All shareholders made an outsized return. The founders became influential executives within the parent company to steer Instagram to newer heights. Most importantly, Facebook instantly gained a massive competitive advantage and increased its enterprise value by far greater than what it paid for the app.

According to the normal laws of business physics, Instagram should not have been worth even a fraction of their final purchase price. Systrom ultimately understood what his company could achieve under the larger umbrella of Facebook. This is why he reportedly asked for $2 billion in his initial bid!

UNCOVER STRATEGIC RATIONALE OF PROSPECTIVE BUYERS, ESPECIALLY IF IT'S AN UNSOLICITED OFFER

It is incumbent upon you, the startup CEO, to learn as much as you possibly can about the acquirer's plan for your company. What are they actually buying? What sort of value will the acquisition create for them in the future?

This is a slingshot moment—one of the points of leverage you have in the negotiation over valuation. If managed well, the results can be phenomenal. But, as is common, founders typically don't scratch the surface hard enough to find out what their startups are *really* worth to the other side. When this happens, you leave money on the table.

Troy Henikoff is a serial entrepreneur and well-known VC in Chicago. He has invested in and mentored hundreds of companies, first through his role as the Director of Techstars Chicago and later as a partner with MATH Venture Partners alongside Mark Achler and Dana Wright.

But before any of this, in 1986, he was a first-time founder with his company SSS (Specialized Systems and Software, Inc.), which he sold to Medline in 1992.

At the time, Troy wasn't planning on selling his company. He and his team were happily building a profitable software company with notable customers like Hyatt Hotels. Troy initially pursued Medline as a potential customer as well and used the software they had just built for Hyatt to build credibility.

In the middle of the sales presentation, then-CEO Jim Mills cut in: "If you can build a purchasing system for hotels, you can build a purchasing system for hospitals— they are just like hotels, only the people don't feel so well." Jim proceeded to make an offer to buy Troy's company on the spot.

"I was totally caught off guard," Troy said. "I had never even thought about selling." He respectfully declined and thought that would be the end of it. A few weeks later, Medline came back with a higher offer price, only for Troy to say no again.

After five or six attempts, the offer number got high enough to catch Troy's attention—a number, he thought at the time, that was too big to refuse. As a young twenty-something entrepreneur, it was the first time someone had put a seven-figure value on his team's work. It certainly wouldn't be the last!

"Looking back, I realize that I did not know the full scope of what Medline's intention was with our software," he reflected. In fact, the company went on to use their now proprietary SSS software to create a new business model that yielded $125 million in annual revenue, a figure that ended up being many times greater than the purchase price of the company.

Without experience or a clear understanding of his value to Medline, Troy undervalued his own company. A price that he thought he couldn't refuse ultimately paled in comparison to the true value he created for Medline.

Imagine how Troy would have negotiated the deal if someone had mistakenly forwarded an email to him about the future plans for his technology within Medline. Your goal is to understand the buyers' business so well that you don't have to hope someone else makes a mistake and forwards you their secrets.

THERE ARE MULTIPLE WAYS TO FIND
OUT THE STRATEGIC RATIONALE

As a founder, you don't have to resort to luck or clairvoyance to find clues to how the acquiring company is valuing your key assets. All you have to do is ask open-ended questions on strategy and shut up. Listening is the single biggest super-power you have during a negotiation. Most will often do the exact opposite and oversell their vision to the acquiring company. All that accomplishes is giving the buyers critical information without learning anything new for your team to use in the negotiation process.

Your job is to understand what the buyer's strategic objective is—regardless of whether they're coming to you or you're going to them. There are a number of nonthreatening questions that founders can ask during the negotiation process to uncover the joint value that you can create:

- What is the long-term objective?
- What amount of funding will be made available after the acquisition? What will this accomplish?
- What will integration look like?
- When will your finance and HR teams enter the conversation?
- What does success look like for you?
- What is the cost of not doing a deal today?

- What are the threats keeping the CEO up at night?
- What will the new org chart/reporting structure look like?
- How will this acquisition impact the current or future share price of the company?

The more freely and openly they answer these questions, the more you can verify their intent. If they can't (or won't) provide answers or they engage in evasive tactics, these are signals that indicate they are far from being able to close the deal.

The bottom line is, don't fall in love with the deal. Once a deal starts to get some momentum, it's basic human nature—and the personality trait of all driven type A people—to drive for success and closure. Don't succumb to the dark side of your eagerness to find closure. Remember that many deals fail. Strive to be as objective as you possibly can be. If an answer doesn't jibe for whatever reason, slow down and carefully, methodically think it through. The most powerful tool you have in any negotiation is the power to say no.

It is also your job to figure out where the pressure points are in the acquiring CEO's orbit. Who are the stakeholders that influence a CEO's strategic priorities the most? After identifying them, you should tailor your strategy accordingly. Start by thinking about the following stakeholders: board members, activist shareholders, former executives, channel partners, and analysts.

Remember that most of what the buyer is paying for is the future value of your efforts. The best price is the one both parties feel is fair and sets up the long-term partnership to succeed. Too high a price, and expectations for return will be unreasonable. Too low, and it is unlikely that appropriate resources will be allocated for success.

IDENTIFY YOUR MOST IMPORTANT ASSET:
TEAM, IP, SALES, TAX LOSS CARRYFORWARD, ETC.

We've established that high valuations are the result of buyers pricing for the future value of a startup integrated into their larger business engine. But how exactly are they determining that value? What exactly are they buying? Part of knowing how to analyze your future value to an acquiring entity is understanding what your main strategic asset is.

The assets of your company can be broken down into familiar key areas: team, leadership, market, growth, technology, and profitability.

Some companies are acquired for the future potential of their proprietary technology. Some are acquired based on a multiple of trailing top-line revenues. And some financial buyers are simply looking for a multiple of EBITDA.

The information you gather in these early stages of negotiation to understand how to best position your company to cocreate immense future value will also help uncover which of these strategic assets will be most valued by the acquirer. While the acquisition is for all of the assets of the company, it is very likely that your acquirer cares way more about one of those things above all else. Knowing this insight is a huge indicator of where the future value lies.

Don Loeb is the former lead of M&A for Techstars. He has advised hundreds of startups going through this process. He stresses that most founders in the technology space are looking at acquisitions that are below $100 million. These sub-$100 million exits are often not the ones that are splashed across front pages or shouted from the rooftops. They may only return 2x or 3x for their investors.

When we asked him the one thing he wished that founders knew, he didn't hesitate for a moment. But what was surprising about his answer was he said it was something that not only founders but also acquiring companies overlooked too often.

"For the majority of these 'smaller' acquisitions in technology, the code base isn't worth much of anything (with few exceptions) without the team as well. It's the people with whom you grinded it out and did the nearly impossible—creating value from a totally new organization and technology where there was none before. That's where the value is," he explained.

Again, it comes down to positioning yourself with your potential acquirer for the highest degree of shared value that can be created together. Understanding where your strategic value advantage lies in the eyes of the acquirer is also important so that you can position those assets in the best possible light.

Simply put, buyers do not want future headaches. And they will zero in on any reason to say no to the deal. If the buyer is interested in a high-functioning creative team that produces amazing products, make sure you take care of any HR issues. If the IP is the big draw, make sure that any and all legal filings are completely squared away. Any perceived employee or IP liability can, and most likely will, come back to bite you later in the process.

SHUTTING DOWN FISHING EXPEDITIONS

Not every offer is a serious one! It's your job as the CEO to snuff out solicitations without real interest behind them. David Cohen from Techstars has direct advice for CEOs who want to distinguish real interest from a waste of time. His simple advice is to ask for the ballpark offer right after engaging them.

At this point, the rule of thumb is simply sharing information on your company that you are comfortable sharing with a future investor. In other words, the information you can share without an NDA. He says, "You can expect questions about revenues, expenses, head count, conversion rates, attrition rates, and all sorts of detailed stuff. Without mentioning an NDA, provide a few high-level answers that you're comfortable with them knowing, and when the questions get into the 'zone of discomfort,' ask them to provide a detailed list of their questions via email so that you can work on them."

After the initial questions are answered, you should ask for the ballpark offer. Now that you've answered just a few high-level questions and have a more detailed list of what they're after, it's important to have a price on the table before proceeding, even if it is a range.

The hard part is to choose your words wisely—you can't be too interested or not interested enough. David shares the following words of wisdom to help the CEOs he works with: "Explain that you've received their email. You're obviously flattered with their interest, and you're happy to answer all of their questions under two conditions. The first condition is that you'd like all of the information that they requested to be covered by an NDA. The second condition is that before proceeding, you would like for them to provide the likely 'ballpark' parameters of the acquisition via a simple email, including the likely cash/stock split."

Most acquirers will happily accept the first condition (not doing so is a serious red flag) but will avoid the second condition. But it's important to stand firm on both before proceeding. The acquirer will likely claim that they don't have enough information to make an offer and that they need their questions answered. Assuming that you've given them basic revenue and expense figures, this is a bluff. Hold firm. Explain that you're very busy working with customers and improving your product and that you can't afford to distract the company without having at least a ballpark understanding of the offer. Explain that it's obviously non-binding and that you won't hold them to it but that you're just trying to determine whether you should discuss this with your board.

Sometimes there is a little dance at this stage, where they will look for a couple more tidbits of information in order to give this ballpark offer. That's fine—use your best judgment. This is your leverage to get the ballpark offer, so don't give it away. Recognize that the NDA won't protect you from giving the "fake acquirer" exactly what they wanted.

If the acquirer resists the NDA or the ballpark offer, they're probably just fishing. You're not being difficult. You're asking a perfectly reasonable question about ballpark deal terms before wasting your time.

People who are not high up enough in the acquiring company to actually be making this offer will be scared off at this point. That's a good thing. Perhaps they never had permission to be pursuing an acquisition in the first place. This technique weeds those people out because they have to provide the nonbinding ballpark offer in writing via email.

TYPE OF ACQUIRER IMPACTS VALUATION

Setting your expectations is the first step to negotiating a FAIR exit that is right for everyone. Accurately setting your expectations starts with understanding the type of acquirer you are dealing with. In Part 1, we explored all the different ways you can be set up to make smart decisions years before entertaining acquisitions offers. Understanding the strategy around who your likely acquirers are and baking in those expectations up front is certainly part of the planning work to be done before you reach the negotiating table.

But there is a notorious Yiddish adage, *"Mann tracht, un Gott lacht,"* meaning "Man plans, and God laughs." Future planning is critical, but once you decide to sell, you have to stay nimble and flexible. If Facebook was your golden target but you have to pivot to other options, make sure you have a handle on how to adjust your valuation expectations.

There are the Big Five, those Silicon Valley giants dubbed with the intentionally intimidating moniker FAANG. This is, of course, Facebook, Apple, Amazon, Netflix, and Google (Alphabet). You can also add companies like Microsoft, Adobe, Oracle, and SoftBank to this list. These companies view acquisition as an innovation R&D pipeline. They are set up with highly professional operations that scout, negotiate, and integrate teams and technology into their larger engines dozens of times throughout the year. These are your all-star acquirers who pay the big 10x tech multiples of every investor's dream.

In terms of valuations, a tier below these Big Five are the strategic buyers within your industry, followed by PE and other financial buyers. Each of these tiers may or may not be realistic for you to consider, but it's worth evaluating all your possibilities—especially to avoid ending up like Troy and undervaluing your company!

Ask yourself if the potential buyer makes a lot of acquisitions or very few. Is it their first one? Are they a public company with transparent financial records or a private entity?

It might be true that your mom thinks your company should sell for $500 million, but if you're looking at a set of potential acquirers who don't play ball in that size stadium, you're going to be off the mark. The trick is to temper optimism with realistic expectations. If you are expecting a huge tech multiple from a conservative industry competitor, you're going to be heading into the negotiation already starting with an insurmountable gap.

After you've gathered as much information as possible, you should have an understanding of your value, what is possible for you in terms of partnerships, and the kind of buyer you want to work with. From there, it's time to agree on the details.

It's time to fill out a term sheet, the most important document in the whole process. Just like how founders shouldn't proceed without a price range over an email earlier in the process, at this point David Cohen insists that founders should not proceed without a term sheet. He writes that "even at this stage, many acquirers will go silent for a long period of time. Sometimes this is normal—these things just take time. Keep building your business in the meantime, and continually push for a term sheet fully describing the acquisition."

Now let's talk about what's inside a term sheet.

CHAPTER 7

WHAT IS A
TERM SHEET?[9]

G ETTING TO THE TERM SHEET IS A REAL MILESTONE. Most acquisition discussions don't make it to the stage where a nonbinding term sheet is signed. There will be lots of discussions over the years to build up a strong rationale that justifies a price both sides are happy with. If this is a FAIR deal, prior to a written offer, you should have had verbal alignment on the vision for the future, the time-line to close, and, most importantly, the final price.

Take a deep breath here. There are many highs and lows in the startup journey, but this is a special one. No matter how you view it, it will be emotional to see a piece of paper that has the potential to create generational wealth. It's okay to be excited, nervous, scared, or determined—we felt all those feelings too.

Despite the verbal promises you've already secured, nothing is real until things are written down. This is the phase when negotiating the particulars of the term sheet kicks into high gear. In order to negotiate well, we first need to learn more about what each of the terms means, what can and should be negotiated, and which points are not worth pushing back on.

When you receive the term sheet, especially if this is your first time, you are going to be experiencing wildly divergent emotions—both elation and fear. The goal of this chapter is to arm you with information so that when you sit down with your attorney, you will have a good foundational knowledge of what the terms mean and what is important. Ultimately, you, as the leader, need to give your attorney the right directions for what to focus on and what not to squander time arguing about.

The term sheet is by far the most important document in the whole transaction, and it is wise to treat it as such. It outlines the key terms of the deal and, done right, will become the foundation for a smooth process down the road. Signing the term sheet doesn't mean you will close the final deal—it is usually nonbinding. However, it is the point of no return as it likely will commit you to negotiating exclusively with one party.

We know the feeling well. It is pure bliss to receive any document that says your startup is worth millions of dollars. The euphoria that comes from that tends to make founders overlook the rest of the document. The term sheet includes a *lot* more than the final price in question. Here is an overview of what you should expect to find in a term sheet:

1. Price
   a. Calculation
   b. Front-end adjustments
   c. Back-end adjustments
2. Closing conditions and timeline
   a. Necessary approvals
   b. Due diligence checklist
   c. Exclusivity and expiration date
3. Personnel agreements
   a. Organizational structure
   b. Governance
   c. Retention tools

THE FUNDAMENTAL DIFFERENCES BETWEEN LETTERS OF INTEREST (LOI), TERM SHEETS, AND CLOSING DOCUMENTS

An ideal term sheet sets the stage for the whole process of an exit. A letter of interest is simply a weaker term sheet with way fewer details, usually only indicating a loose timeline and price.

The closing documents are outlined in the term sheet, and they get drafted once the term sheet is signed by both parties.

While the M&A term sheet looks similar to a financing term sheet, what's inside is completely different. For the definitive breakdown of a VC financing term sheet, we recommend Brad Feld and Jason Mendelson's excellent book that has stood the test of time, *Venture Deals*.[10]

The M&A term sheet packs a punch in terms of the amount of detail in it, and you should want it to—this is how you get full visibility into the material terms of your deal. Generally speaking, there should be no surprises, good or bad. Most often, the buyer will schedule a call in advance to walk through the key points and confirm that everyone agrees. It's a practice that solidifies trust for both sides. Needless to say, founders should never sign a term sheet they don't intend to finalize with closing documents. A signed term sheet means all the focus now turns to reflecting the agreed-upon terms to binding closing documents. If the deal falls apart afterward, bridges are burned.

As a buyer, Gary Johnson always anticipates which parts of the term sheet the founders won't like. He is a huge proponent of transparency and understands that the perception of a surprising negative term is likely a lot worse than what it actually means. More importantly, he believes that explaining why a term needs to be in there ahead of time helps founders get rid of this terrible feeling: *Am I getting screwed?*

In 2019, Atlassian made a bold, unprecedented move for a seasoned acquirer. They published their standard M&A term sheet publicly and, in doing so, shared with the world what mattered to them most and, most importantly, why it mattered. (You can still see the term sheet itself if you search for the Atlassian term sheet.) Their efforts toward transparency should be highlighted and followed for everyone making an acquisition in the future.

Unfortunately, there is no standard set of documents companies use for acquisitions becuase every situation, company, and strategic rationale for doing the deal is different. Picking one apart isn't necessarily going to help the majority of the situations you could find yourself in, but it is worth familiarizing yourself with the general outline of information.

Instead of publishing a term sheet, we decided it would be much more helpful to share a framework of terms and questions you should familiarize yourself with before accepting your first term sheet. Our goal is to be as generic as possible here so that you can apply the details of your exact situation when the time comes. Then, the more details the term sheet can include, the better.

Remember, as time goes on, the ability to negotiate dwindles, and the pressure to close increases with each passing day. The negative feelings that accompany any concession can tank the deal as a whole. Not to mention that changes after the term-sheet stage are not cheap. Once you are into due diligence and the drafting of definitive agreements, the legal bills increase exponentially for any modification. Our recommendation is to negotiate the term sheet in earnest and, as long as the terms are FAIR, sign it with the intention of closing the deal. In this stage, there are three main components in the term sheet you should pay attention to: price calculation, certainty to close, and personnel agreements. Here's what you need to know about each of them.

THE HOLY TRINITY OF M&A TERM SHEETS: PRICE CALCULATION, CERTAINTY TO CLOSE, AND PERSONNEL AGREEMENTS

Entrepreneurs should use these three buckets as a mental framework to define what matters to them: price, certainty, and personnel. Signing a term sheet and going into exclusivity with one party means you are forgoing the option to remain independent, raise additional capital, or evaluate other buyers. The details need to make sense!

The worst term sheets are skinny letters of interest—they only indicate price or, worse, a price range in consideration for the purchase. This is rarely the starting point of a FAIR deal. The buyer should have already discussed the rationale, integration plans, and internal alignment needs with the seller; therefore, there should be no issues putting down the important points that frame your deal. Remember that whoever drafts the final documents (most often the buyer) sets the terms. You have maximum negotiating leverage before you sign the term sheet. What's not inside this document is likely going to be buyer-favorable in the closing documents.

Typically, the term sheet will be accompanied by a cover letter with a few paragraphs on the rationale for the acquisition. This is as important as the document itself because it confirms the document was drafted with the ultimate objective: to actualize the goals embedded in that rationale. This is the moment that will prove that the buyer has thought carefully about the deal and that negotiating will be done in good faith. After all, the shared objective belongs to both parties, and both of you should be motivated to make that happen.

The first thing anyone wants to find out is price. Let's dig in.

Price Calculation

This is always a surprise for less experienced founders; the commonsense approach is to expect a simple number: "We are buying your startup for $100 million!" If only it were that simple.

The purchase price is never just a number; it is always accompanied by details around the adjustments and tax implications. For instance, when your startup is acquired, you will likely have some amount of cash in the bank. What happens to that money? Does the acquirer "refund" the money by increasing the purchase price accordingly?

The first part of understanding price is to understand how proposed figures are calculated.

Point price versus a range: There is a huge distinction between companies acquired by a flat number versus purchases where a price range is defined with a formula to calculate the specifics. The first is easy: we are buying you for $X. This then becomes the starting point for the rest of the document.

The alternative is used for companies where the value increases over time. For instance, a company growing 10 percent month over month will double its customer base in a year. In such a fast-paced environment, the price can be defined as a range depending on certain milestones—such as a multiple of revenue on closing date. This is simply a copout on the part of the buyer; all it says is that the buyer hasn't completed the due diligence in full to commit to a price.

Our preference is that the number should be a point price at the high end of the value of the strategic rationale of the deal. This makes everything simpler and maximizes the return for all shareholders.

To avoid confusion, this is different from an earn-out scenario. An earn-out is similar to paying in installments; it means that the buyer is committing to future payments to shareholders if certain conditions are met. This is commonly reflected as a fixed price plus an earn-out based on a formula.

This usually happens if there is a difference of opinion on the current value of the startup—an earn-out can bridge the gap between the buyer and the seller.

Cash versus stock mix: Cash is exactly what it sounds like, a huge sum of money sent via wire transactions by a paying agent. However, public companies can offer to pay for the company in the form of their publicly traded stock. If the markets like the transaction, this will drive the company stock price up, essentially paying for the whole acquisition in certain instances.

There are two ways of pricing stock in a deal: fixed ratio (you get X shares, fixed when we sign) or fixed price (you get $X worth of shares at close, where the number is determined based on the buyer's closing price). The distinction is important because you are much more prone to the market reception of the deal in the first instance (fixed ratio), and the second protects you from the market reaction, assuming the deal is announced at signing (as most are).

This also aligns all parties in working to drive up the value of the company. Essentially, all new employees have their net worth tied to the buying company for a certain "lockup" period where they aren't allowed to sell. That can be annoying for sure, but imagine the awesome feeling if the stock price doubles in the period you worked tirelessly to make the acquisition a success!

Of course, it works exactly the reverse way as well. If you don't evaluate your buyer correctly, the millions of dollars the company is sold for can evaporate into thin air during the period you aren't allowed to sell your shares. Mark experienced this personally when his first company, the Whitewater Group, was acquired by Symantec. At first, things seemed great—when the deal closed, Symantec stock was trading at forty-eight dollars per share. All he had to do was wait ninety days as part of the lockup period.

Unfortunately, in that period a scandal broke, indicating that the CEO of Symantec might have committed a crime. In front of his eyes, the stock price tumbled to six dollars per share when the lockup period was over. It was painful and taught him a valuable lesson about not counting money before the deal is completely closed. As often as possible, stick to cash if you aren't absolutely willing to take risks.

Valuing buyer stock: This is another important detail in pricing because a public stock price is never a fixed number. Typically, a weighted average of the last ten to twenty days is used to determine the share price at the time of closing.

However, all bets are off if the buyer is a privately traded company. This is where negotiation takes over. The buyer will argue that the stock should be priced at their latest round, a premium on the latest round, or even a future valuation at which the company will eventually go public. The seller will argue that the price should be determined by the fundamentals of the company today. This is really hard to get right, and the winners and the losers are separated by a mile. Getting acquired by a company like Google, Facebook, or Twitter in their early days, where a secondary market already existed, was at least more helpful. These companies were so valuable before going public—with valuations well into the billions—that there were whole marketplaces for investors to buy these stock options. However, what if Theranos was making the offer? Their public fall from grace would mean that the proceeds from the sale would also get decimated in value. This isn't so far from the truth: just a few weeks before WeWork's very public fall from grace, they were in serious acquisition talks and had already bought a number of companies using their stock.

Ask yourself this: do you see yourself working to make this private company as successful as possible for the CEO who is making the decision to invest in you? Ultimately, the belief in the value of a private company is tied to the belief in the mission and the talent of the people pursuing that mission. If something in the stock offer doesn't feel FAIR, call off the deal altogether instead of negotiating the amount. Remember, you are effectively "investing" the value of your company into theirs, much like a VC would invest cash.

Finally, pay extra attention to when the stock is priced to determine how many shares will be used to purchase the company. For longstanding public companies, this isn't so much of an issue. It's the younger, more volatile companies where the number can fluctuate wildly, as well as in situations like the crash of 2008, where the bottom of the market seemed to fall out.

This is a good place to use the analysts from your investment banking team to run a few scenarios.

Tax treatment: If stock, is it "tax deferred"? This is a massive point to highlight, especially for you and your team members. Unless structured properly, the stock component that you receive in a deal may be taxable to you. That means that whether or not you receive any cash in the deal, you have to fork over to the IRS the amount of tax on the gain represented by the stock portion (and any cash portion) of your deal! This can have a serious effect on what you actually take home when it's all said and done.

Make sure you understand the tax implications of stock payments. For cash deals, this is much simpler.

Earn-outs: In addition to the retention incentives to employees of the startup, buyers may offer future payments if certain milestones are met. It's extremely important to understand the conditions around these payments. Timeline and milestones are the two key components. What objective needs to be achieved in what period in order to receive earn-outs?

The most common milestone is an increase in revenue, typically calculated with GAAP principles. However, we have seen other metrics make their way into this calculation, such as EBITDA, FDA approvals, or technical integration of existing platforms. The most important component is to make sure you understand what you are signing up for. Avoid people- and retention-based milestones. Most often, these terms are useless and set up the company for the wrong incentives. Ultimately, the buyer is in charge post-closing and can have extreme impacts on both retention and people. Remember that objectives like EBITDA will be much harder to predict and control once the documents are signed. After all, it is the acquiring company's accountants who determine how expenses are allocated, and that can tank an EBITDA easily.

Understanding share price calculation: How much will each share be worth?

Once the dust settles and there is a final price on the company, the way you will determine who makes how much is simple. Divide the full purchase price by the total number of shares, and you get a price per share. Multiply the number of shares you own by the share price, and you are all set.

However, you must understand what is on your capitalization table and what is included in your total number of shares. For instance, technology startups typically have an employee retention pool of shares. These belong to no one until they are awarded as an incentive. What happens to those groups of "unassigned" shares? This can be as much as 5–10 percent of the whole price! You can argue that those shares should be left out of the calculation of the price per share—this can move the dial significantly.

You should also pay attention to how the per-share price is calculated and make sure it is done in accordance with the "treasury method." Put simply, this has to do with how options are treated in the deal. Commonly, they will be "cashed out" based on the net spread between the per-share price in the deal and the exercise price so that option holders don't need to reach into their pockets to pay the exercise price. However, if you don't add the aggregate amount of those exercise prices to the deal price to come up with a notional per-share price (to take into account that the buyer will pay less for an option than they will for an actual share), the buyer will end up paying less than the headline valuation in the deal. This aggregate exercise price can be in the millions, so it's worth clarifying this point with your legal team!

Front-End Price Adjustments

By now, we hopefully have a number to work with. The next exercise is to agree on the conditions where that number will be adjusted. Don't think of this as a renegotiation of the deal; there are simply not enough known details about your startup to work into the price.

Debt: This is a downward adjustment of price. It is there to prevent behavior like borrowing a million dollars the day before the close and passing on that obligation to the buyer. Sometimes debt is in the form of a convertible note from a past raise; it can also be a bank loan against receivables. Be careful to avoid loose definitions of debt here; buyers can include things like the operating lease of the offices in this area, so ask for clarification to avoid surprises down the road. Remember that since the convertible debt likely converts at a sale, you need to double-check the terms beforehand. This will impact the purchase price in a material way.

Cash: Simple enough—usually the cash in the bank at the time of closing increases the purchase price by the same amount. (As a side note, this is another reason to run a profitable business!) However, this is not always the case, and buyers can request to keep the cash or argue that offshore or restricted cash needs to be treated separately.

Working capital adjustment: Most startups need a minimum amount of working capital to keep running their operations. The spirit of the term is to avoid situations where the buyer immediately needs to infuse cash in the business after the close. This would effectively adjust the purchase price, and the goal is to avoid surprises once again. Conversely, if the target's trajectory is good and perhaps there are some nice customer deals on the horizon, a working capital adjustment could act to increase the price paid. Be mindful of whether the adjustment is only one way down (in favor of the buyer), or a two-way adjustment.

This is potentially big, as it can include terms like deferred revenue adjustment. It is not material for every business, but if you are running a large-enterprise SaaS business with long implementation cycles, you might have millions in deferred revenue from accounts waiting to go live with their purchases.

Finally, you must pay attention to the timing of working capital adjustment. It is unlikely that the financials will be official on the day of closing—this typically takes sixty to ninety days. In certain cases, both sides can agree on estimates and course correct afterward—this is called a two-part adjustment.

Transaction expenses: These are all of your expenses related to the closing; typical items are legal and investment banker fees. However, you might have to clarify items like double-trigger severances, stock acceleration for certain employees, or payroll taxes.

It is always a good idea to double-check the thought process behind these adjustments. Buyers acting in bad faith might view these tools as ways to reduce price later in the process. That might work for one deal, but over the long term, it ruins the reputation of buyers from a FAIR standpoint.

Back-End Price Adjustments

Even when the price is agreed upon for the day of closing, we are far from being done with the final number. Fair warning, this is a really complex part of the term sheet, and you will want to go over it with your lawyer twice.

These are the clauses that last for years after closing and can impact the purchase price to the point of clawbacks from sellers (in extreme situations). Think of this as insurance on the deal. It's a minor expense if nothing goes wrong, but in the event of catastrophe, the adjustment can be massive.

Escrow: This is where you define how much of the deal is at stake if any of the promises are broken. Think of it as extremely expensive insurance; typically 10–20 percent of deals are held back for twelve to twenty-four months. The riskier the acquisition, the higher the amount and the longer the period. In the research phase of this book, we saw ranges all the way from 5 to 25 percent, so this is a point of negotiation, and FAIR deals will benefit tremendously. The elements in a FAIR deal reduce risk by design.

Pay extra attention to deals where your equity revests; this means that the buyer is using the share of your proceeds as a tool to retain you. There may be tax implications, and you have to double-check what you are actually going to get paid on the day of closing after taking all of these deductions and oldbacks into account.

Indemnification: If the escrow is the amount of money in the insurance policy, think of indemnification as the conditions for the payment: it simply states the promises you are making and who is responsible for the bill if they are broken.

You are effectively giving a backstop to the representations you are making, such as the correctness of the payout spreadsheet, existing litigation, and pre-closing taxes owed. There are a whole host of adjustments that can come back to haunt you, sometimes with strange terms, such as liabilities using open-source code or export controls around violating any sanctions. Each of these representations and warranties (promises you are making) has a different survival period and can come back to haunt the shareholders.

For instance, a heavily negotiated item here is indemnification from IP matters. The buyers will want all of the risk to be absorbed by the shareholders; if the company is infringing on any IP and gets sued for it, the payment held in escrow can be used for legal bills. The sellers will argue that all IP infringement (known or unknown) is too broad, and it is virtually impossible to "prove" that the company isn't infringing on any IP. All items that go in the indemnification section should be clearly outlined and negotiated, with the grand assumption that the due diligence is wrapped up with no issues. If there are specific concerns or liabilities discovered in the due diligence process, those will be directly deducted from the purchase price, or the buyer will amend the indemnification to include them.

Survival period: This is important because it is how long your obligations will hang out there for. Most of the general representations on the company will be for twelve to twenty-four months because buyers will want to go through at least one audit cycle. Coverage on items like intellectual property can easily extend from eighteen to thirty-six months, and fundamental representations survive for much longer, often six to ten years.

Fundamental representations: These will be much more carefully defined, but understand that things like cap table management or issues with problem shareholders will (and should) be your responsibility for a long period of time. For instance, if the CEO has exceeded their authority by signing the deal without the consent of the board or the shareholders, the buyer will expect to be protected against the fallout. As long as the process was FAIR, this is usually not something you need to worry about.

Liability cap: This is exactly what it sounds like: the maximum amount of exposure for the sellers if things go wrong. This is typically just the escrow amount for general representation breaches. In specific cases like intellectual property breaches, it can be more than the escrow.

Taxes and fundamental representations go to the full purchase price, and if you commit fraud, the sellers have the right to ask for their money back (and potentially more!). There is a much higher bar to prove wrongdoing, but an uncapped liability means that the buyer can come after shareholders—including you—for damages. These caps are highly technical in how they work together with the escrow amount, and you should clarify hypotheticals with the M&A team while going over the term sheet.

Baskets: Given how comprehensive indemnity provisions can be, this language is used to protect all parties from every small issue becoming a legal matter. Think of this as a sort of "deductible" on your insurance policy: a threshold under which claims are deemed too small to deal with. The basket can be for individual claims or a combined aggregate where claims add up to a certain amount before they are addressed. These range from 0.25 to 1 percent of the purchase price.

NET OPERATING LOSSES (NOLS)

This is another area where seasoned founders who understand their businesses in their entirety can have an edge. NOLs are simple—you have likely been operating your company unprofitably for a number of years, accumulating a bunch of losses along the way. This is essentially taxable income, and late-stage companies can use a portion of your losses immediately as a tax write-off. (We are assuming that your buyer is likely a profitable company that pays income tax.)

There is a complicated accounting study to determine how much can be used, but for startups that have raised significant capital, this number can be a material increase to the final price.

Our recommendation is to leave this point to assess separately. NOLs can be significant, so you don't want to be "guaranteeing" them as part of the indemnification obligations we talked about earlier. However, if they are valuable to the buyer, then you may have an opportunity to negotiate additional value for them. Either way, it's a complex analysis and nuanced point to negotiate, so you need the thoughtful guidance of your lawyers here.

DEFENSE COSTS

This is a point that gives a lot of undue heartache to all parties. The question is: who picks up the legal tab if there is a third-party lawsuit in connection with this acquisition? This is a broad point, and the lawsuits have to be directly tied to your representations and warranties.

The most obvious one is around the intellectual property claims. If you get sued by someone who believes you are infringing on their patents, the buyer will be stuck with the legal defense costs. Even if the accusers are no more than patent trolls, the legal costs can add up quickly with large companies, prompting a settlement. The buyers will look for an agreement that doesn't include a "knowledge qualifier;" however, it's in your best interest to keep the language. The difference is that with a qualifier, the buyers will have to prove that you knew there was an issue and you hid that evidence during the acquisition discussions. This is a high bar to clear, and that's why buyers almost always want to remove this language.

Their argument will be that this lawsuit would not have existed without the acquisition, and it won't matter if you are infringing or not or whether you knew about it or not. In their minds, either way the legal costs are your responsibility. You will argue that the very reason patent trolls are coming out of the woodwork is because the bigger company is a target with large checkbooks. If there is infringement your investors should pay. If there isn't, the buyer should pick up the tab.

This point can go either way, and it all depends on whether the buyer is open to sharing the risk around future problems. Legal bills are costly either way—better to pay your M&A counsel to get these points right than to pay the buyer's lawyers to dispense with claims later!

Rep and warranty insurance: Since we have been using the insurance analogy, it is only natural that some companies have switched to buying actual insurance policies to get rid of much of the indemnity structure altogether.

This makes a lot of sense to us! These insurance products have been around for a while, and are heavily used in the

PE industry. They are not widely adopted by strategic tech buyers, but companies like Atlassian have already made this their standard. There is a deductible like all insurance products, usually 1 percent of the purchase price, and that is much better than a 10–20 percent escrow. The premiums are usually 3–4 percent of the coverage limit, and both the premium and the deductible can be negotiated to be split with the buyer.

Here is the actual language from the Atlassian term sheet blog post[11]:

Escrow and Insurance

As partial security for Atlassian's post-Closing indemnification rights, an amount equal to 1% of the Purchase Price (the "**Escrow Amount**") would be held in a third party escrow fund for 15 months after the Closing.

Atlassian would obtain a representations and warranties insurance policy ("**R&W Insurance**") in connection with the Proposed Transaction. The premium, taxes, commissions and any other fees and expenses payable in connection with obtaining R&W Insurance coverage for a policy limit of 4% of the Purchase Price (the "**R&W Insurance Expenses**") would be paid for by the Sellers.

All of this leads to our ultimate number; once all the deductions are done and the ranges are solidified, we have a number from which to begin the rest of the process. However, just like a financing round, the price is only a third of the battle. There are two more important buckets of items that the founders need to pay extra attention to.

CLOSING CERTAINTY

Who cares about a $100 million price tag if the deal has lots of uncertain conditions and risk? This is one of the easy parts to overlook—the price negotiation can be tense, and less experienced founders assume that the internal alignment and closing conditions are relatively straightforward. During Mert's deal with SwipeSense, he recalled thinking, *Why would they bother putting all of this work in if the internal alignment wasn't there to begin with?* But it does happen, and because it is a possibility for you in the future, we want to make sure you're prepared. Here are a few details to pay attention to in your term sheet when the time comes.

Buyer approvals: Of course, in FAIR deals, alignment around the approvals happens much earlier than the term sheet. You should look for language in the term sheet that confirms the expectations from both sides. If they are silent on the conditions of closing, below are a set of questions to ask the M&A team in the review conversation:

- Does the term sheet have the support of the right people in senior management? Are there any naysayers who can veto the deal? Who is the ultimate approver?

- Has the buyer's board reviewed, socialized, and approved the transaction? Especially with public companies, this is critical.

- If this is a large acquisition by a public company, their large shareholders will need to vote on the deal to approve it. What are the expectations around the process? Have the shareholders ever turned down a deal?

- What are the key conditions to closing?

It is important to note that all of these approvals, even in writing, are given with the expectation that due diligence won't uncover skeletons in the closet.

Key due diligence items and timeline: The first item to clear away is the type of due diligence the buyers will require—is this confirming what you already know, or will you use the due diligence to determine the final price of the company?

This is extremely important; if the buyer is "guessing" the value of the company, you shouldn't have made it this far in the process. The rationale behind the deal needs to be supported by data, time, and relationships—the amount of work required to perform the full due diligence is enormous. For a founder, this isn't worrisome because the buyers may find something they shouldn't; rather, you should worry that the company is going to be extremely distracted during this process. This is what makes signing a term sheet the point of no return; don't go into a complicated due diligence process without having the full intention to close the deal.

It is always a good idea to put a rough timeline in the term sheet, as well as a list of material due diligence items. The exclusivity period and the time it takes to complete due diligence can be different.

Exclusivity period: As we iterated earlier in this book, time is not your friend when it comes to the actual sale. The elements of FAIR need time to mature; however, putting in all this time in advance has a goal of accelerating the process at this stage.

Buyers will want the reassurance that you won't shop around the deal to other buyers for a certain period of time. Hopefully, the partner you are negotiating with is truly your FAIR home so alternatives aren't on the table. This isn't always the case, so make sure that you are agreeing to a period that you can honor. Remember that the other options will likely be dead and cold after this period. No one wants to play second fiddle to another company.

To avoid tension, it is important to define the circumstances that will extend the exclusivity period. Be wary of evergreen definitions of exclusivity, meaning that the period would continue indefinitely until one of the parties gave notice to the other. IBM made this term popular, and it doesn't sound as bad at first—all you have to do is to give a heads-up to let the other side know you aren't extending.

However, in practical terms, this sounds awful—like you are walking away from the deal or you are going to evaluate another offer. This will likely upset your counterpart and, unfortunately, damage the deal. This is why it is best to clarify and avoid evergreen terms in general.

Most of the exclusivity language we reviewed includes financing the company in any shape or form because raising a large round typically competes with selling the company. However, there will be instances when the shareholders might need to float the operations for a few more months to close out the deal. These are referred to as the bridge rounds, and buyers will have no problem with them as long as you disclose the purpose and the amount ahead of time.

Finally, it is expected that if the buyer behaves in bad faith, such as changing the price or another material term, the exclusivity will be voided. This detail is critical to address, and you should probably move on from the acquisition altogether if there is bad faith on either side.

Closing conditions: Apart from timeline and process, there are hard requirements unique to each deal that will need to be checked off before the closing. It is rare to have all of these spelled out in the term sheet unless the seller has tons of leverage. Regardless, it is in your best interest to ask questions pertaining to the actual criteria for the close. Here are some examples of the various kinds of conditions:

- *Antitrust and Other Regulatory Approvals:* The bigger the acquisition, the bigger the risk that the FTC or DOJ will have something to say about it. This can be massive, and if there is a material risk associated with antitrust, it is typical to see reverse break-up fees (the amount of money sellers receive if the deal falls apart due to antitrust concerns) in the deal.

- *Bring-Down Standard to the Representations and Warranties:* This means that you need to be clear about what will constitute a breach of promises such that the buyer has the right to walk away. Not all errors are malicious; for instance, it's common to see a handful of shares get miscalculated from one spreadsheet to the next. How will the closing documents define the range of the error? Think of it as defining the reasonable approach to an error—you don't want to throw the baby out with the bathwater over every small issue.

There are three kinds of standards to inquire about that clarify the effect of an error:

- ○ Material Adverse Effect: This is the most common standard and one you should push for. It essentially means that there was a big problem to the tune of 25–30 percent of an important number like revenue. This is the standard public companies use in their acquisitions because the cost of a deal that falls apart due to technicalities like this one is massive.
- ○ Material: This is a much lower standard, think 5–10 percent. This is known colloquially as the "get me out of the deal" standard—it will be trivial to find some documentation that has this level of an error in it. It isn't impossible to see, but it should raise an eyebrow.
- ○ Flat: This is the toughest standard; it means everything is correct to the most absolute term possible. This is virtually impossible to guarantee— what if there was a $10,000 calculation error in one option for one employee? This gives buyers a huge amount of leverage—essentially a right to walk away from the deal anytime.

- *Employee Conditions:* The next section will go into detail on these, but the buyers might require a certain percentage of employees to sign their new employment agreements before closing the deal. Again, in a FAIR deal, this is not an issue because your teammates should be thrilled with the exciting new vision for their future. However, it is wise to avoid putting the fate of the deal in the hands of a small group of employees who may not be privy to every step of your exit journey.

• *Stockholder Approval Thresholds:* This is the percentage of your shareholders that will need to approve the transaction—typically 85–95 percent. Common perception might be that only 51 percent of the shareholders need to approve, but this creates risk for the 49 percent if they do not agree to the indemnification provisions of the deal or if they decide to sue the acquirer down the road. This requirement for such a high percentage can put a lot of leverage into the hands of very few; be careful if you have dissident holders, ousted founders, or shareholders in other jurisdictions. The best way to avoid issues here is to eliminate dead equity on the cap table as much as possible; these are the shareholders in your startup who are no longer adding value. As long as the shareholders are informed, this should only be a mildly frustrating exercise of chasing down signatures.

- *Third-Party Consents:* You might be under contracts with your customers, licensors, or suppliers that require them to sign off on the transaction before it can proceed. Ideally, these provisions are rare, but a very typical place to find them is in your office lease. Landlords have been known to stick up closing, for instance, to negotiate higher rents. If they are key licensors or customers, they might require better terms before they consent.

- *280G Approvals:* This is another point where we will ask you to double-check this with your lawyer because things can get complicated. The IRS has a complex tax rule that essentially states that if you are making too much money too fast, you might face an extra 20 percent in taxes.

  The formula to determine whether you qualify for this bracket involves your past three years of earnings and the full disclosure of the amount you are making in closing. The top employee earners in any deal typically qualify for this, including the founding team.

  Now it's not the end of the world—you can be exempt from this tax if you convince 75 percent of the noninterested voters to approve the 280G vote (this means that you can't vote for it if you are going to benefit from the vote). You also aren't allowed to combine this signature with the closing documents; your shareholders can vote no here and approve the deal.

Needless to say, issues arise when all shareholders are sent a notice that includes the past three years of earnings and the exit proceeds of a handful of employees. Note that the employees (current or former) who aren't making as much also get to see those numbers, and that can cause quite a bit of tension internally, especially in situations where shareholders or disgruntled early employees who have an axe to grind against the top earners get involved. Translation: you can get totally screwed over this point or be forced to pay an extra 20 percent in taxes if you aren't careful.

- *Governing Law:* Finally, understand the governing law for the whole agreement. Certain jurisdictions are more friendly to sellers; certain ones are advantageous to the buyer. This is a point to clarify with your lawyer. Aim for the neutral playing ground, but know that sellers will usually have little to no leverage here.

PERSONNEL AGREEMENTS

The first item we covered is the price, and while it impacts everyone, it's the most important element to your investors. The second item was the certainty of closing, which similarly impacts everyone, but your board of directors cares most about this point.

The final element impacts the deal as a whole, but it is specifically focused on your team members. You're going to see details around all the HR-related issues born from the acquisition in your term sheet. A company, above all, is a group of people working toward a shared goal and needs to be taken care of and accounted for as such.

The rationale dictates the goal, but motivated talent must be surrounding the objective to make sure it is successful. Let's now explore the many ways personnel are impacted with the acquisition.

Organizational structure: The integration plan defines the ultimate structure that works best for the strategy; this is another instance where there is no "one size fits all" approach. There are instances where it makes sense for the company to stay independent and others where it makes sense to fully integrate the company and restart as a division within the new parent. FAIR deals will have this answered before the term sheet. Gary Johnson likes talking about integration before the term sheet for this reason. The ultimate objective is to understand the right strategy to win together.

Parallel to the structure, the term sheet ideally defines reporting and governance requirements of the company. You should know the objectives of your new manager and the new business unit—after all, they are your objectives now—along with your existing milestones ahead.

This is also where you see the brass tacks of what is going to happen to your team. Will everyone get an offer? If there are redundancies, there are key questions to answer: who will be let go after the exit? What will be their severance payments, and who will pick up the tab?

Retention incentives: There are usually three parts to this construct. The objective is simple: allocate enough resources toward motivating the team once the deal is done.

- *Revesting Equity:* This means that the equity vesting clock is reset for certain deal proceeds, usually only for key members of the team. Understandably, this is frustrating for founders and key employees. They worked hard for their equity and, in certain cases, walked away from cash compensation to earn it. While this is a "stick" approach, unfortunately, it happens regularly, and it is imperative to understand the new vesting schedule and the acceleration triggers. For instance, what happens if the buyer changes their mind in ninety days and decides to fire these key employees without cause? It is unlikely, but this is why it matters.

- *Go-Forward Incentive Pool:* This is the pool of money the buyer allocates to motivate the team. Think of it as a separate increase to the price for those participating; the money here is not for all shareholders but just for employees. As a founder, you should clarify details on what happens if people leave. Can you "recycle" their incentive for others? This can be cash, stock, or a mix of both. For simplicity purposes, think of this as the "carrot" approach.

- *Unvested Equity Assumptions:* If there is a significant retention value in the target's unvested options or other incentive equity, that could mean the buyer is already getting meaningful, inherent retention built in. To simplify incentives moving forward, the buyer can just choose to keep things as they are by assuming the unvested options directly.

Regardless of where the chips fall, make sure to negotiate these three items in conjunction with each other. The objective is to find the right mix where the buyer feels confident the team is here to stay and you, as the seller, feel like you are getting a fair return.

Key Employee Conditions: Retention of a small group of the management team—usually the founding team and senior leadership—is often a closing condition. This is as black and white as it gets: they must be in their chairs as a condition to closing. If this is the case, who these folks are must be defined so there are no surprises. Since this is a closing condition, it is critical to have employee agreements and other arrangements sorted in parallel with the definitive closing documents. Later on, we will dig into the importance of having individual counsel to make sure this doesn't hold the deal hostage. The last place you want to find yourself is standing between "everyone getting paid" and "no one getting paid."

Technical Employees: Sometimes there is a separate bucket for engineers if that team is crucial to the success of the company and the product. Depending on the size of this group, it's not unusual to see a threshold of 85–90 percent "acceptance" rates of offer letters. This book is written with technology startups in mind, but this can apply to any specialized set of skilled employees who are hard to recruit.

Rest of the World: Once the key leadership and technical teams are sorted out, you have to clarify if there are expectations on acceptance letters from the rest of the team. The objective is simple: of course all parties want to make sure the team is happy and productive in their new home. The question is who is responsible; if there is a high threshold of acceptance, the success or failure of the deal is on your shoulders.

If the buyers are comfortable leaving this until after the close, this means that they are responsible for retaining the team in the long term.

Salary and Bonus Structure: Most term sheets will have language around new employment packages—namely, that they are going to be equivalent or better to what people are currently getting paid. This is usually what ends up happening; startups typically have lower salaries on average than established companies. Don't expect offer letters for the whole team (unless it is a closing condition) until the final documents are signed.

Always remember that titles matter a lot more in established companies than startups. Prepare yourself to fight just as hard for titles because larger companies often determine pay grades by title. The difference between a title of engineer and senior engineer could be worth tens of thousands of dollars in stock compensation. It is your job as leader of the company to thoroughly research how the acquiring company uses titles and pay to ensure that your team is adequately compensated.

Relocation: It might sound small, but there are many examples of how this issue ends up tanking deals. The buyer might have an expectation that everyone works under the same roof and will need to outline their plans here. It is fair to push back for resources to make sure the relocation process is smooth for your team members.

Noncompetes and Nonsolicits: This basically means that an employee leaving the company will not be allowed to work in the same space or solicit the existing team to leave and join them. These are highly contentious and might not even be enforceable in states such as California. A direct conversation with the counterpart is also required to understand expectations here—make sure there is clarity around scope and duration. Even defining the timeline can have variations, such as being measured from closing date or date of leaving the parent company.

Waiver of Double Trigger: Finally, the acquirers can require the team members to waive their acceleration rights. This would apply for instances where the employees have agreements for their current roles that outline what happens if the company is acquired. Single trigger means that no matter what happens, all unvested stock becomes yours the second the company changes hands. Double trigger means that all unvested stock is yours if the company changes hands and the buyer doesn't offer a similar or better role to keep you as part of the team. Waiving these rights certainly puts the power in the buyer's hands, but it will come at the price of a deeply frustrated team from day one.

THE CHECKLIST OF KEY TERMS

We are not your lawyers, and we didn't write this book with the intention of replacing legal professionals. As we discussed in the key stakeholders chapter, you definitely will need the support of a reputable firm and, in particular, an M&A specialist who has been through the trenches before. This should definitely not be their first term sheet, and their experience with how this document compares to previous documents will be invaluable.

Here are the top terms you should ask your lawyer and the buyer representative to explain to you. This is our guidance on what terms matter the most and ones that likely won't matter. Once again, think of this as a cheat sheet for quick explanations—you should most definitely understand every single item on the term sheet to avoid leaving millions on the table.

1. Price
   a. Calculation
   b. Front-end adjustments
   c. Back-end adjustments
2. Closing conditions and timeline
   a. Necessary approvals
   b. Due diligence checklist
   c. Exclusivity and expiration date

3. Personnel agreements
   a. Organizational structure
   b. Governance
   c. Retention and incentive arrangements

This is to arm you with information so that you can receive the best advice from your attorney. Assuming you have a real expert working for you, you must listen with humility to their sage advice while having a firm grasp of what is important and really worth fighting for and what are the minor points that you shouldn't waste cycles and dollars fighting over.

Avoid falling into the pit of the "average" term. Each deal is unique, and it makes a CEO look amateurish if you push back by saying your terms are different than most. Instead, work on understanding why a term is different than average, and make your arguments based on that core difference.

Above all, don't sign anything until you are confident you understand and agree with each part of the term sheet. This is your future and the future of your company.

CHAPTER 8

HOW TO MAXIMIZE VALUE THROUGHOUT THE PROCESS

ONGRATULATIONS! YOU HAVE A TERM SHEET IN hand. This is the point of no return. You have selected your dance partner, and you're moving forward into your future with the makings of a FAIR deal. While a term sheet is not a final guarantee that a deal will happen (nothing but the actual closed deal will guarantee that), this stage should be the moment of spiritual alignment. This is an important step, but there is still a long way to go. Throughout the process from a signed term sheet to money in the bank, there are still many ways to either drive greater value or screw it up.

But the term sheet is an important milestone that means there is a real commitment on both sides.

Once you have signed a term sheet, you should act—and assume that the buyer will act—in good faith. From this moment forward, all parties should be trying to close the deal, and momentum will be building toward completing the transaction. If you are not ready to make that final commitment, you shouldn't sign the term sheet. It's that simple. For instance, if the buyer finds out that your company has a lawsuit looming over it that wasn't disclosed, they have every right to walk away given that you did not act in good faith. If there are any skeletons in your closet or issues that an acquirer should know about, you are always better off being the one to disclose them rather than letting the acquirer discover them on their own through their due diligence. Always. It will come out eventually, and it will only erode trust if they feel like you are withholding information.

This also includes technology and security audits. In today's world, IP ownership and a tight security infrastructure really matter. Don't wait until the end of the deal to do a thorough technology audit. If it's going to blow up the deal, isn't it better to find out sooner and save both time and money?

THE DO'S AND DON'TS OF USING A BANKER DURING NEGOTIATION

Our recommendation is that the CEO be the point person on negotiating, but we also realize that not every CEO is a master negotiator. If negotiating is not your strength, or if you want to have someone else take point on a particularly difficult conversation, it certainly is valid to have someone else lead the process.

Personal relationships and trust will often solve problems that can only be handled by the key stakeholders. When SurePayroll was negotiating their sale to Paychex, the personal relationships between the executives of the two companies smoothed troubled waters. After the term sheet was signed and the deal almost done, it came to light that SurePayroll still had outstanding payments to collect from customers that would carry over post-transaction and become Paychex's responsibility. If Paychex did not successfully collect, that money would be taken out of the escrow—meaning that less money would eventually be paid back to the SurePayroll shareholders. This outstanding issue created an impasse at the final stages of the deal. Neither side would budge from their position, and the long sought-after deal was in jeopardy. Crucially, at this point in the process, it's important to understand that this was not simply SurePayroll's problem. Paychex needed to acquire SurePayroll as much as SurePayroll needed to be acquired by Paychex.

The CEO of Paychex stepped up to the plate, looked Scott Wald, the Chairman of SurePayroll, in the eye, and promised they would collect the money. They shook hands. The deal closed. Paychex honored their commitment, and no money was ever taken out of the escrow. According to Scott Wald, who recounted this story, "We met at a hotel bar, and he looked me in the eye, and I felt enough trust was there to make the deal go through."

If you outsource your negotiating, you might maximize your return, but you also will limit trust-building and lose these types of opportunities.

Creating the legal framework that would mandate Paychex using their best efforts to collect the missing invoices would have been time-consuming and difficult to do. Even in the event that was made possible, auditing the effort would have been nearly impossible given the complicated process of collections. Trust made the difference in moving forward, and it all worked out in the end.

This dynamic is not possible without personal relationships involved, and those are something you cannot outsource.

The largest determinant of whether or not to use a banker is related to the size of the deal. If the deal you are negotiating falls below $75 million or so, it's likely not going to warrant using investment bankers. At that size, the potential payout for the bankers won't be large enough to attract the interest of A-level players—and at that point, less-than-stellar talent can hurt rather than help the negotiations.

But assuming your transaction is large enough to warrant using a banker, what is the best way to use them from this point forward? How can you make sure to get the most bang for your buck? One advantage of using a banker is that they see many more deals than you will and have a better understanding of market norms. They earn their fees based on the final price of the sale, so if your goal is to maximize every penny you can, a banker's interests are perfectly aligned with that goal. Having a banker negotiate the hard deal points allows you to "preserve" your good relationships and not have to be drawn into possibly contentious negotiations that could impact future personal relationships. Remember, this is the company you are potentially going to work for post-transaction. It is sometimes helpful to have a barrier between the two parties if, but more likely when, things get heated.

On the other side, every single corp dev leader we spoke to dismissed bankers and wished they weren't there. Yes, this is self-serving because they think bankers drive up the price and make the negotiations harder. That being said, most CEOs don't know how to manage their bankers, and as a result, bankers can drive too hard a bargain by setting unrealistic expectations. Bankers can also "protect" the CEO too well and get in the way of the CEO forming the necessary personal relationships. The worst reason for a deal to die is that a banker has essentially cratered it.

At the end of the day, it's up to the CEO to manage the bankers, the process, and the final negotiating points. The more you understand where your hard lines are, the easier it will be to give directions to your banker.

MANAGING YOUR LEGAL TEAM TO MAXIMIZE EFFECTIVENESS AND REDUCE COST

Assuming, of course, you heeded our earlier advice and paid up to hire experienced M&A attorneys, this is the point that will pay off. While they will have a team to support you, in general, you should work with the most senior attorney on key strategic questions. While one hour of their time will be expensive, their insights and wisdom can cut straight to the point and save you both time and serious money over the long run. In addition, have your data room in good working order before you start this process. Nothing will rack up unnecessary legal fees like having highly paid lawyers tracking down unsigned contracts.

You should have a conversation with your senior attorney ahead of time about prioritizing issues and risks. Your attorneys' job is to manage risk and save you from yourself. However, not all risks are created equal. Some attorneys will fight equally as hard for the minor points as the major ones.

It is critically important to work out a process with your attorney ahead of time and a framework for decision-making to help classify and understand the level of risk on any particular item. Know what is worth fighting for and what isn't.

Lawyers work for you, and it's up to you to determine what the important business priorities are. Jason Seats, Chief Investment Officer of Techstars, emphasizes this key point when counseling entrepreneurs. He said, "You cannot outsource judgment to the lawyers."

You should avoid having your attorney negotiate a major deal point on your behalf with the opposing attorney—at all costs. One way to quickly tank a deal and rapidly escalate tensions and costs is to have two attorneys going back and forth over major deal points. We cannot emphasize this enough: major deal points should be negotiated between you and the appropriate business champion on the other side if at all possible. Business unit leaders should be negotiating business terms; lawyers should be negotiating legal points.

Lawyers hate to put caps on their fees for obvious reasons. Asking them to do this before a term sheet is in hand won't generate an effective estimate and won't endear you to your legal team. They simply don't have enough information to be able to accurately provide a number for the cap without knowing the details. However, once you get to this point, a seasoned M&A attorney should have a pretty good sense of how much time will be needed to close a transaction. If you can, now would be a good time to negotiate a cap on their fees.

In truth, everyone hates paying legal fees, and many feel like their legal fees were too expensive post-transaction. Most lawyers know this angst exists but urge the business community to consider the difference in attitudes between paying a lawyer or paying a banker post-transaction. No one seems to mind paying their banker the fees (typically substantially more than the lawyers), but everyone hates paying their legal bill. If Kahneman and Thaler have taught us anything, it's that humans are predictably irrational. Yes, the legal bill stings. But there is real value there.

So do yourself a favor. Hire the best M&A attorney you can find. Follow these guidelines. Be judicial in how you use and manage them. And then take comfort in the knowledge that you made the best decision and were smart and justified in getting the representation you needed to make this deal happen.

ONE VOICE TO RULE THEM ALL: ONGOING ALIGNMENT

Corp dev professionals manage transactions every day. You might do it at most a handful of times in your life. There's a good chance you're reading this because you're about to go through your first one. There is an asymmetry of experience between you and the buyer.

For instance, one thing you'll see as you navigate your first exit (and hopefully the others after) is the divide-and-conquer technique of corporate development leaders. The buyers will constantly probe for differences in opinions between the board, CEO, and other key executives—even different classes of shareholders who have different financial motivations and timelines. They will ask the same questions multiple times to multiple stakeholders to see if the answers vary at all. The more they understand key differences, the better they may exploit them to negotiate a better deal for them and a worse deal for you.

It is critical that you have only one person, ideally the CEO, be the point of contact and the only person responsible for negotiating. Deals can quickly go off the rails when multiple people are talking. Let's revisit Anne Bonaparte, the CEO who has successfully led six companies through exits. During one of these transactions, she said, "I had a VC investor who was on my board and thought he could negotiate a better deal. And he reached out directly to the acquiring company without my permission!" She continued, "Of course I found out about it and just thought it was a real shame and made us look desperate. I think ultimately this little move cost us maybe millions off the sale price in the end."

Get your ducks in a row. You need to have an explicit conversation with your board, your investors, and your key employees on what they can and cannot communicate or say.

We promise that being thoughtful and proactive about communication with your internal stakeholders ahead of time will save you a lot of pain. You might not have as much experience as some of your investors, but having a singular voice for the company will save you headaches down the road. There can only be one voice. You need to step up, have a direct conversation, and assert your authority if that voice is yours.

The more clarity you have—and can communicate with authority—on where you draw the line, the more effective and impactful the negotiation. You should also expect this same level of clarity from your buyer. The sooner both sides understand their respective nonnegotiable points, the faster you will get to a decision. If something is truly nonnegotiable, don't be afraid to express it up front. A fast answer—especially a quick no—is always better than a long, distracting, and expensive process.

COMMUNICATIONS WITH BUYERS AND YOUR TEAM: INFORMATION ASYMMETRY, INTEGRITY, AND ALIGNMENT

We are big believers in empathy. The more you know about the people who are sitting across the table from you, the more you care about their success. And the more you genuinely care about their success, the more successful you will be.

Most CEOs sit back and wait for the acquiring company to tell them why they are interested. We vehemently disagree with this common course of action. There is a fundamental information asymmetry between the larger acquiring company and you. Your job is to fix that. You both must learn everything you possibly can about the other's company, but you have to help build and craft the rationale for why this investment makes sense to the acquiring company.

Rishad Tobaccowala, former Chief Strategy Officer at Publicis, said that larger companies are "process driven" while entrepreneurs, by necessity, are "instinct driven." That means that the larger company has a formal evaluation process. Understanding that process will help unlock how they think and what is important to them.

Rishad also believes that larger companies are not looking for incremental improvements. If buying your company will result in an incremental gain, then they could build it themselves. Larger companies are looking for game-changing, step-changing, real impact. Your job is to make that case.

So how do you do it? Hard work and research. Start with corp dev. Remember every conversation is bidirectional. Start asking questions about their strategic objectives. If possible—and every company is different—find the business champion and build the business case for strategic impact together.

Pro tip: if the acquiring company is publicly traded, then go back and start reading about and listening to their quarterly earnings call and find out what the company is reporting on, what promises they are making about the future, and what questions the analysts are asking and tracking. The analyst can actually be a fantastic resource—go and have a conversation with them about what they are looking for and what they think about the future of that company.

Bottom line: do not wait for them to tell you the greater why; do not sit back and let them run the show. Remember that deals can and often do fall apart even after a term sheet, especially when there is a lack of alignment in telling the greater strategic story. The key to alleviating tension is communication with cadence: regular standups as part of the purchase process.

Creating structure, engineering a process, and overcommunicating all take valuable time. Time that's worth spending. There are always problems in all deals. With a standardized communication process, there are expectations and trust that help ensure accountability and remove any unnecessary fear or doubt about games being played. In the absence of knowledge, basic human nature is to assume the worst in the other party. Don't let doubt fester. Keep regular calls with each important stakeholder so that no conversation ever feels too dire. You will feel neither desperate nor secretive if each conversation is planned weeks in advance.

This is a key part of Atlassian's strategy as well. Sarah Hughes, Director of Corporate Development, quickly figured out this secret as she was first getting started. M&A deals are full of emotional turmoil and rough patches. The best way she has found to make sure these inevitable bumps in the road don't derail the deal is to make a daily five-minute check-in meeting with the founder sacrosanct. "It's a nonnegotiable part of my process now," she said. "There's no getting around the fact that you have to be in constant communication every single day while you are in the period between issuing a term sheet and closing."

Startup Communication Strategies with Key Leadership and Team

By their very nature, deals are often secretive. While you are meeting with your lawyers and bankers and running the deal, your team is hopefully running your business. You can't be two places at once, and you need to trust that your team is holding down the fort. One important reason that deals can fall apart is if the seller's business loses any momentum during the due diligence process. If progress slows down for any reason, the acquiring company is going to investigate, which could lead to second-guessing their purchase.

Each CEO will handle this differently, and there is no single correct approach. We tend to err on the side of making sure your key executive team knows what you are doing and how you are spending your time. Just like you have built a regular cadence of communication with the acquiring company, we think it's equally important to provide your executive team with regular updates on your progress. Once again, in the absence of information, human nature is to fill in the blanks and sometimes assume the worst. Confidentiality is key here, and you have to set the expectations up front that your team will not share any of this.

As far as the rest of the company is concerned, the rule of thumb is to keep things confidential until you see the finish line. As you go through due diligence, certainly key members of your technical team will get involved in explaining your tech, as will some members of your finance team who will be part of the transaction. Word gets out, especially on smaller teams. Ultimately, it's your decision, but our recommendation is once you are at this juncture of a signed term sheet, you probably will have to tell your full team.

Remember FAIR. Lay it out for them. Set their expectations carefully for what it will mean for them. People will be nervous. They will have questions that they expect answers to. They'll want to know if they're losing their job, if their position is changing, if they will gain financially from the sale, and many more questions.

We think the Golden Rule applies. How would you like to be treated? What would you like to know if you were in their position? Never commit to anything you can't deliver, but remind your team that you are advocating on every shareholder's behalf, including theirs.

TACTICS TO KEEP MOVING FORWARD

Identify the business champion to negotiate on the startup's behalf.

Every acquiring company is different, and each will run a different process. With some companies, the transaction will be CEO led. With others, it will be the corp dev team that identifies and leads the transaction. Still other companies will be led by their product teams. For example, at Apple (in most cases), it's the product manager who identifies and leads the deal, while at Google, it may typically start with corp dev. At PayPal it's the corp dev team that leads the strategic charge. Your job is to understand the culture and process of the acquiring company and identify your key business champion. This is critically important when negotiating.

And we've said it once, but we'll say it again: business leaders should be negotiating key business terms—not attorneys. You will need your business champion for every step of working through FAIR. And it will be your business champion who will help you build out the case and lead you through the inevitable rough patches. When the moment comes—and it always does—that you hit an impasse, it will be the trust and personal relationship you have built up with your business champion that will inevitably carry the day. This is when you call in the champion. When you hit the proverbial wall and you can only negotiate so far, your business champion becomes your advocate. You can only use them once, maybe twice, so pick your moments. But don't be afraid to ask. Leveraging their internal goodwill and trust at a key negotiating point can be the difference between a deal getting done and not.

Create a Sense of Urgency to Drive Timeline

Keeping the ball moving forward can be difficult. Hopefully, you are negotiating from a position of strength and are ready to sell at the optimal time because you want to and not because you are running out of money. The journey of a deal can be maddeningly slow, with fits of activity and moments where it looks like nothing is happening. If you are the CEO, this can be extreme torture. Stay calm and true to your path, and be proactive whenever possible.

While your options may be limited because larger companies are going to have to work through their process, you do still have some weapons at your disposal. Remember this is not about you—it's about them. This is where radical empathy comes in. Pleading to get a deal done sooner will most likely have the opposite effect. This is the moment for rationale to come shining through. Consider these questions:

- If this is a game-changer that will allow the buying company to grow market share, what is the opportunity cost of waiting?

- If there is technology work to be done to integrate the two product lines or finish up features, how much are you leaving on the table by delaying?
- If there are outside analysts looking for this functionality or competition who already have this, how will your internal sales team react when they don't have this in their portfolio?

Repeat after us: *rationale, rationale, rationale.* The more the acquiring company believes in the deal rationale, the more urgent their actions will be. In addition, they will be motivated to work through the problems to maintain the closing timeline.

Due Diligence is Bidirectional

Information is power. Every single time you have an interaction with the buying company, there is an opportunity to learn more about them. Now that the term sheet is signed, the buying company will begin due diligence in earnest. They are going to explore every nook and cranny of your business. Nothing will go unexplored, so be prepared. This is also the time for you to be doing your own due diligence. Think of it as preparing for a job interview.

After all, this will be your new employer. Going back to our FAIR model, this is the time for you to be actively exploring cultural fit: understanding their corporate decision-making structure to help build their internal case for alignment, preparing the mutual integration plan and, most importantly of all, refining.

Whatever you do, don't sit back and let them manage the process. You need to be just as proactive in gathering all the information you can to help build the case and continue to reinforce and push the sale through. Now is not the time to stop and rest on your laurels. Momentum is good, but momentum alone won't get the deal across the finish line.

CHAPTER 9

HOW TO KEEP YOUR CALM AS THE CEO

ET'S TAKE A MOMENT TO APPRECIATE HOW INTENSE this all is. Negotiating your life's work is never easy or simple. It is emotional and volatile. Your job is to recognize the situation for what it is and be intentional about creating practices and surrounding yourself with people that help you ride out the storm.

Almost every individual we spoke with, no matter their role, pointed to the importance of keeping yourself together. Conflict is inevitable. Tension is everywhere, but your job as a leader is to stay calm. Don't panic. Project confidence. Even in the moments you want to curl up into the fetal position and hide in your bed, you must project confidence for your team, stakeholders, and buyers. You will get through this, one way or the other. We promise.

There are a few important tactical tools to greatly reduce tension and frameworks to help you work through issues. Keep in mind that bigger problems begin as small problems. The more proactive and in control you are, the more you can resolve conflicts before they grow too large. Always keep the long-term view in mind, communicate clearly, and continuously align with each stakeholder.

THE IMPORTANCE OF A MENTOR OR BRAIN TRUST

You need people in your camp who have been where you are. Even better if they have been where you are *and* have ended up where you want to go.

If this is your first transaction, having a mentor or brain trust to call on is absolutely critical. But even if this is not your first transaction, be assured that even the pros need an inner circle of trusted advisors, if for no other reason than to remind you that you aren't losing your mind.

In *Thinking in Bets*, PhD psychologist and champion poker player Annie Duke writes her treatise on the psychology of decision-making. She notes that brain trust groups of trusted advisors help make us "more successful in fighting bias, seeing the world more objectively, and, as a result, we will make better decisions. Doing it on our own is just harder."[12]

Not only is the middle of a transaction emotionally fraught, but there are, of course, legal ramifications and confidentiality issues at play. You may feel pressure to isolate yourself with sensitive knowledge to protect against a worst-case scenario of information getting leaked. But you cannot navigate the stresses of this time by yourself. So yes, you must have at least one person (but hopefully a couple of people) who you can trust to the core. They can be a board member, an investor, a co-founder, a fellow CEO, the right legal counsel or banker, or even/especially a spouse or life partner. There will be inevitable crises where their experience will come in handy. But you also need them for the day-to-day gut checks: "Is this normal? What should I expect? How would you handle this?"

When Mert was in the middle of his transaction selling his first company, SwipeSense, he was eventually able to put together such a brain trust that ultimately helped him feel secure enough to close the sale. On the other hand, had he had trusted mentors in place at the very beginning of the sale process, it might have reduced some of the personal heartache that can, and often does, accompany this process.

Mert started SwipeSense from scratch when he was still a student at Northwestern and continued building up to its exit in March 2020. It was really his first job out of college, and with it he experienced many important "firsts," including his first acquisition.

There were many times during the transaction process that Mert felt cornered and alone. He experienced times when he was sure the deal wouldn't close and everything that he had worked so hard for would come crashing down. These moments of despair are inevitable, and he now realizes that he would have benefited greatly by having someone he trusted early on to help keep him calm and give him perspective.

Of course, Mert wasn't alone in the deal; he had lawyers, bankers, co-founders, teammates, investors, and a board of directors. But each of these had competing incentives, and he felt inhibited in how he could discuss and present his challenges.

Ultimately, it was his responsibility to surround himself with people wiser than himself, and that's what led to the ultimate success of his transaction.

YOU'RE NOT ALONE–THIS IMPACTS YOUR FAMILY AS WELL, SO TURN THEM INTO A SOURCE OF STRENGTH

It's an incredibly long road to the final transaction—don't expect a FAIR deal to happen in the first five years of your journey. For most of us, especially first-time entrepreneurs, we've risked everything, skated by with dicey health insurance, and sunk every penny of savings into our business. If you have a spouse or life partner, let's just say this hasn't gone unnoticed.

Mark's first software company, the Whitewater Group, was just getting going when his first daughter was born. His wife, Marcie, who worked at the company making calls to collect licensing fees, would often take the baby to work and balance a crying baby in one arm while on the phone with a delinquent customer. Startups are often a family affair, and they have just as much at stake as you do.

The stresses of a startup are real. The stresses of working together with a significant other in a startup are a force multiplier. It can certainly work, and there are many successful examples of happy life partners and happy work partners. For Mark, three weeks into having his wife work in the company, he asked her to do something (Mark remembers this in the most polite and respectful way), and she threw up her hands and said, "You're not the boss of me!" and left with their baby in tow. Clearly, in that case, it was helpful to have separation of home and work.

Regardless of how involved a spouse is with the day-to-day business, they are involved in the exit. Spouses play an integral role in these situations because they have the most to gain—but equally, the most to lose. And they often have paid a dear price thus far to support the founder in the endless and tireless pursuit of making their startup a success.

Recognizing where significant others can help and where they can hurt is also a part of managing these critical relationships. One banker told us a story about a company that received an offer for $30 million. The spouses of the founders were ecstatic. They had cartoon eyes filled with dollar signs and started to spend the money in their heads. The banker felt the price was too low and convinced the founders to keep on pushing. The spouses were upset and strongly urged the founders to sell immediately. Turns out the banker was right, and the company, after some back and forth, ended up selling for $70 million.

Selling a company is incredibly stressful on you, yes, but also on your partner. Often there is an information asymmetry because you are living it in the moment and have way more information than your spouse does. Be sensitive to their position and their feelings of lack of information and control. And enlist their help and support—if nothing else, their emotional support. Remember, you are in this together.

STAY CALM, EVEN, AND LIKABLE—
EVEN IF YOU FEEL LIKE LOSING CONTROL

When the world seems like it is crashing down on your shoulders, remember this too shall pass. Throughout the book we are hammering on the importance of building trust and having a long-term view of your important milestones. This is the moment when it comes into play.

All deals have bad moments. Miscommunications happen that drive our inner demons to assume the worst. The glue that holds it all together is personal trust. We can't tell you enough how important it is to earn a reservoir of trust to call upon in these moments. Trust enables you to give the other side the benefit of the doubt. Trust is the lubricant that gets the machinery going again.

Equally important is your ability to adopt the mindset of a long time horizon. While this might be your first, it is likely not your last exit. You have the rest of your life in front of you. Post-transaction, you will be wiser, with some hard-fought wisdom, a little scar tissue, and the intellectual and capital resources to do some real future damage. How you act today matters. Your reputation is everything.

When Cliff Shaw sold Mocavo, it was the result of a number of lessons he learned in his previous—and, to his mind, failed—transaction attempts with earlier startups. One of the big lessons he learned was to manage the optics and keep his cool no matter what. In a pivotal moment in his transaction, the banker from the acquiring company called to share that their side had serious concerns about the readiness of Mocavo's technology to scale.

At that moment, Cliff was seeing red. Cliff responded in a calm but firm way, "If you insult my team again, we are going to walk away. Is this the kind of long-term partner you are going to be? Is this your culture?" The banker backed off, and the deal proceeded. Cliff was grateful that he was able to think critically and calmly in that fateful call.

The relationships you forge will hopefully be with you not only in this transaction but the many more to come. In the process of writing this book, we interviewed corp dev leaders from many large companies. When looking at their LinkedIn profiles, do you know what they all have in common? They all did corp dev for multiple companies. The person across the table from you today may very well be across the table from you for your next transaction—and they all talk to one another.

So stay calm. Don't fly off the handle. Be in control of your emotions (at least publicly). Don't burn any bridges. Use the twenty-four-hour rule. If you think something you are going to write or say might be controversial, give yourself twenty-four hours and the night to sleep on it. Or use the *New York Times* rule: never say anything that you wouldn't want to become a headline in the *New York Times*. Whatever the frustration, remember that the way to work it out is *with*—not *through*—the other person. And most importantly, assume good intentions until proven otherwise. Maneet Singh, who works as a corp dev manager at Facebook, likes to say, "Modulate the paranoia."

And while you're at it, try to maintain equilibrium and a good sense of humor. Human nature dictates that we want to work with people we like. To the extent you can, try to be pleasant. Crack a smile or be in good humor. It can't be fake.

Everything you do has to be authentic to you. But remember, this is also a job interview of sorts, so don't be an asshole (unless, of course, that is authentically who you are, in which case it might be helpful to hire a banker to hide behind!).

PRACTICE AND PREPARATION: PRACTICE MAKES PERFECT

Ask any banker, and they will tell you that M&A is both an art and a science. Turns out that there are best practices and guiding principles to managing a process. Gary Johnson told us that "empathy is the most important skill set to have in any transaction." So be curious. Ask a ton of questions, and remember the answers you are given. Do what you can to understand the other point of view, and use it to help you remain calm and focused.

One of our favorite games to play during these stressful times is "what if?" model it out. If you can anticipate problems, you can be prepared with answers. The more you practice for possible outcomes, the calmer and more at ease you will be when they happen.

Cliff Shaw and his wife spent time together running through scenarios, generating likely questions, and practicing answers. It was this kind of muscle memory that helped him react in the most advantageous way possible in the moment.

One of the common ways founders get tripped up is when corp dev professionals make the move to casually throw out a floater balloon of a number—something along the lines of, "Given market conditions, a purchase price of X seems reasonable, right?" How you answer that question is critically important and can literally mean millions of dollars in your pocket.

Some tools you can use to practice are:

- Role-play different situations.
- Write people cards that list personality traits and behaviors to expect.
- Learn your lines. Practice how you are going to answer potential questions *ahead* of time.
- Build a habit of requesting information whenever you are asked for information. It's always a great practice to ask why someone is asking for a specific piece of information or acting in a certain way and to get in the habit of asking for reciprocating information.

FOUNDERS' PERSONAL COUNSEL

Negotiating your personal employment agreement can either be an extreme source of stress or an easy-breezy process. One element you can't ignore is the potential conflict of interest between what is best for you and what is best for the shareholders and the acquirer.

Obviously, you want to be happy, and it's also rational for the acquirer to want you to be happy. Interests are aligned there. But the devil is in the details. For instance, it would be much more preferable for you if the key employees walked away with their full proceeds from the exit. For the buyer, it is much more preferable to have all of your earnings tied up to continuous employment or future performance. The reality is that it will fall somewhere in between, depending on how well each side negotiates.

A few pieces of advice here: first, if there isn't a straightforward agreement on what you are looking for, get your own HR counsel. Ultimately, the M&A lawyers are working for the shareholders, and they can't give you advice that will jeopardize the transaction. In other words, they will be working hard to reduce risk from the deal as a whole versus protecting your interests.

You are an executive who is being courted to join another leadership team; therefore it's completely expected to have your agreement reviewed in detail to make sure you understand what you are agreeing to. And the little things matter. For example, it's likely that at the larger company, your title will matter more than at the smaller startup, as larger companies tend to tie titles to compensation levels.

Second, don't leave reviewing and negotiating your own employee agreement—and those of your employees—until the end. You do not want to be in the uncomfortable position of being the person holding up the rest of the deal from moving forward. Putting yourself in this position will build up pressure and urgency to "just accept and move on" to close the deal. But "hoping things just magically work out in the end" is no strategy at all. Before the deal is done is the time when you have the most sway and negotiating power.

Use your good relationship with your board so that your investors are positioned alongside you as allies in asking for what will be good for the founders and the team. Brad Feld, entrepreneur, author, blogger, and venture capitalist at Foundry Group in Boulder, Colorado, emphasizes this point in his speaking and writing on the subject: "If you have a good relationship with your investors, address it with them at the beginning of the transaction. Collectively agree to be aligned throughout the process, with each of you reinforcing messages to the buyer about this alignment."

This is important, especially in situations where the buyer wants to go around the cap table and allocate more consideration to employees, or when the transaction is modest and the common stock and options receive little consideration. If you are aligned with your investors on how to approach things, what is fair, and where you both want things to land, it's much easier to negotiate with the buyer with one voice.

Collin Wallace, the CEO of FanGo and angel investor, raised this point from his personal experience with his first exit. Grubhub, the acquirer, wanted a longer than typical vesting schedule for Collin. As a result, "I tell any founder who asks me for advice to hire a personal attorney," he said.

Remember that the company attorney represents the company and all shareholders—not you, the CEO. Collin went out and hired his own personal attorney, who then fought for the contract he wanted. It's really important to keep in mind that your company attorney does not work for you: they work for the shareholders. Sometimes that doesn't matter, and sometimes it can be the difference of millions of dollars in your pocket. Brad Feld agrees: "Founders should always get their own counsel. Company counsel does not work for the founders but for the company. There will always be a moment in the transaction where the company's goals and incentives will not be aligned with the founders'. This doesn't have to be a contentious moment, but having separate counsel makes it cleaner to work through."

You have a lot more leverage now to make sure you are all in. It doesn't help anyone to close a deal with frustration on either side, and that brings us to the final point.

DON'T GO TO BED (OR CLOSE THE DEAL) ANGRY

Do you view life and transactions like a zero-sum game where winning is only defined by how much money you make, to the exclusion of others? Is your complete focus on maximizing this transaction without thought to further opportunities down the line? Do you plan to not be a part of the acquiring company or leave at the first available moment? If yes, congratulations! You're an asshole. We wish you well and hope to never be sitting across the table from you in a future transaction.

Collin Wallace told us one of his biggest inspirational texts for entrepreneurs is the book *Finite and Infinite Games*.[13] "That book is my model for how I think about operating in business and life," he said. "I think for entrepreneurs to be successful in this business we have to understand the point of the game is to keep on playing, not for the game to end."

And so if you don't already, we must insist that you consider the value of personal relationships. If you want to start off on the right foot with your new company, it's a good rule of thumb to try to craft a deal and manage a process that, in the end, maintains the integrity, trust, and goodwill of the people who participated in the transaction.

PART 3

CLOSING AND INTEGRATING FOR THE FUTURE

That's it. You've kept your cool throughout the tension and negotiated in good faith for a deal you are excited about, and finally, the term sheet is signed from both sides. This is a great feeling, and it is definitely a moment to celebrate.

At this point, everyone around the table is hoping for a straightforward process to get the transaction across the finish line. As long as the closing documents reflect what is on the term sheet, the majority of the shareholders should approve the transaction, and the deal will formally happen.

While most signed term sheets result in a closed deal, that doesn't mean a deal is done by default. As we know, in life, shit happens.

Just because you are here doesn't mean you are across the finish line—far from it. Keep in mind that if the deal falls apart, little changes in the buyer's world. Sure, some people might lose their influence or get a negative performance review, but life goes on.

In your case, this could be the end of the journey. This is not a friendly period; the deal is vulnerable to changes in the market, your performance, and everything in between. Until the documents are signed and the payment hits your bank account, you need to be ready to call it off if things aren't progressing as expected.

Let the lawyers focus on the legal points while you efficiently work through the business issues. Know that the teams you have hired get paid regardless of the deal closing, so the incentive to close needs to be driven by the business stakeholders.

The following chapters are your step-by-step guide to getting the deal closed while preparing yourself for a successful integration. This is the final grade on the acquisition. It all comes down to how well you can integrate your people, product, and profits.

It is your responsibility to take care of your team when the dust settles, both in terms of them getting their fair share as well as their roles in the parent company. There is a sacred trust between you and your team, and this is the true test to make sure you go to bat for them.

Life on the other side can be wonderful, and this remaining part is to show you how to get there. A FAIR process will pay its final dividends here; you are set up for a smooth close and a new beginning under a new umbrella.

CHAPTER 10

HOW TO GET FROM A SIGNED TERM SHEET TO THE CLOSE

N THE DOZENS OF INTERVIEWS WE CONDUCTED IN the making of this book, not one of the founders' transactions went perfectly smoothly. There are always bumps in the road. We heard about an investor who was named as part of the Mueller investigation during the Trump presidency and had all their assets frozen, the federal government unexpectedly saying no to Comcast acquiring Time Warner Cable, inept or overreaching attorneys putting deals in jeopardy, and everything in between. There are always unforeseen challenges that can sink any deal, no matter the size.

Unpredictable circumstances can come from anywhere. You can focus all your time and attention on a transaction, and before you know it, you've taken your eye off the ball. Your company starts losing customers or misses a key technology deliverable. There can be rogue investors or board members who have their own agenda or key employees who have you over the proverbial barrel to sweeten the deal for them.

A pause in the deal proceedings might have absolutely nothing to do with you. The acquiring company could have a CEO change (happens all the time), and the new CEO could have different priorities. Your business champion can leave the company. You may fall on the wrong side of internal politics between competing camps from the acquiring company. Or simply, the acquiring company's priorities may shift for whatever reason.

Forget your company or the acquiring company. Challenges can come from external threats like a stock market crash, government regulators, or natural disasters. For crying out loud, who saw COVID-19 coming? Let's face it: life is messy.

A healthy dose of paranoia is welcome at this stage. A FAIR deal is elusive to put together and easy to lose without focus. Let's delve into some of the things that can go wrong between a signed term sheet and the closing day.

UNPREDICTABLE MARKET CIRCUMSTANCES MAKE DEALS FALL THROUGH

At this point, the most common reason for things to steer in the wrong direction is simple: the buyer essentially changes their mind; the deal doesn't make sense anymore. This could have nothing to do with your performance. The issue is that the buyer is going through a crisis. Maybe their stock price is taking a hit, or there is controversy in the media. Remember that in the month leading up to Adam Neumann's very public collapse as CEO of WeWork—and the immediate reversal of the company's fortunes—they had been in active talks with a number of smaller companies to acquire them. Suffice to say, those deals did not close. And there was nothing those startup CEOs could have done to change the outcome. It's important to keep in mind that there are forces beyond our control.

It takes six to eight weeks for final documents to mature for signatures. For simpler technology deals, this is much faster. Employees and complicated ownership structures slow the process down. The deal is vulnerable in this time period; essentially the assumptions that gave way to making this deal possible need to stay constant right now.

While it is impossible to predict the future, it is possible to align on expectations. Understand your rationale inside and out, and ensure that the buyer is in a stable period.

CLEAN OUT THE SKELETONS IN THE CLOSET—
THEY CAN COME BACK TO HAUNT YOU

Startups are messy. Lack of experienced management, lack of time and resources, and sloppy management show up in different ways. This is nothing to be embarrassed about. Rather, it's something that the founders need to start fixing as early as possible in the process (and in a transparent manner).

This is part of what can be a painful discovery and due diligence process. You will go a long way to ensuring your deal closes by meticulously listing all of the open-source libraries used in the product, ensuring that all enterprise customers have signed agreements and renewal contracts, cleaning up employee documents to make sure everyone has transferred their IP rights, having employment agreements in place, maintaining a consistent shareholder structure, and keeping well-documented shareholder agreements.

We discussed the importance of the data room and why it matters to keep it organized as part of good management practices. Even with the most experienced management teams, it is understandable to have things fall through the cracks. It is okay to have skeletons in the closet as long as you are transparent about the problem and act swiftly to resolve it.

What happens if you discover that an employee from a long time ago never completed their separation agreement? As a founder, you might be inclined to look the other way and hide an embarrassing blunder. Surely, the legal team isn't going to be stuck on one signature. Trust us: they will.

When you uncover an issue like this, no matter how small, make a big deal out of it. Bring it up in the daily standup as something you just discovered. Be honest. Talk through exactly what you are doing to track down the solution, and take the problem seriously. This will likely lead to the buyer softening up on their requirements instead of the other way around. If a corporate development executive senses that you are avoiding the issue, they will double down and hang the agreement on your ability to track down an elusive signature. No side wants to have a problem down the line, and it is critical to have a clean sheet in the beginning of the relationship.

We can't emphasize this enough: a missing signature from an offer letter, an incomplete customer contract, and other seemingly small details can tank deals! It's not that the buyer is worried about the employee walking away or the customer canceling the services. It indicates that there are bigger secrets that the founders are hiding. Whether this is true or not, perception is reality.

Facebook's policy is to walk away from deals if these kinds of issues are discovered during due diligence. For instance, a routine step in every diligence process is to list out each employee and their immigration status. Compliance with employment laws is a much greater liability from the buyer's perspective, so any missteps here are a huge deal.

Imagine if a buyer signed a term sheet with a startup that had one employee who was still working with an expired H-1B visa. Even worse, what if the founder knew about this problem and had actively decided to not disclose it ahead of time? If you can't trust a leader to be forthright with issues, how will they fare inside their new home? Will they also sweep problems under the rug, hoping that they never escalate? The point here is that the immigration challenges would not have been a deal-breaker; after all, seasoned buyers have swarms of HR pros who can fix the situation. The issue is lost trust. As we pointed out earlier, once the trust bank account is withdrawn, it stays empty for a while.

Don't put yourself in this situation. Keep your closet organized, and if issues arise, overcommunicate. Deals die because of undercommunication, rarely the other way around.

LOSING A CHAMPION TANKS MOMENTUM

This is an even tougher one to swallow: what if your executive champion suddenly decides to leave or, even worse, is fired in the middle of a transaction?

There are two key stakeholder relationships in every deal that must be preserved from start to finish: the business unit leader and the executive champion. Consider the startup sale as the ultimate business-to-business deal in the company's history. The business unit leader is the user, and the executive champion is the buyer. Without one, the other is useless. A buyer won't risk the capital with subsequent execution; a user won't have the clout to get a deal done without purchasing power.

Long-term relationships come into play here; you are trusting your buyer-side counterpart with your destiny during the sale process, and you deserve trust and transparency. A buyer with integrity won't begin a process if they are on loose footing, and you shouldn't be working with executives who don't know they are in trouble to begin with. These kinds of issues are easy to mask short term, but a long-standing relationship will breed the trust to have an off-the-record conversation about where things stand in the world of the buyer.

Fundamentally, this is about alignment. If a stakeholder departs the process unexpectedly, call an all-hands with the remaining stakeholders from the buyer's side. Ensure that the deal is still on, and give them space up front if they decide to back away. You would much rather pause the process now and let things settle down than force the deal through without the stakeholder. The missing stakeholder is either immediately replaced by another executive from the buyer's side, or they weren't necessary to begin with. It is a huge red flag to see inaction from the buyer's side on this.

You might also find that through the process, you lose allies on your own side. If a rushed process leaves you out of alignment with your shareholders and they go rogue, things get tricky. A disgruntled investor who is refusing to sign the closing documents in protest can cause much bigger issues down the road. It is entirely possible that the investor could reach above the CEO directly to the buyer, signaling their discomfort. It will be much easier for the buyer to walk away at that stage to avoid a future lawsuit; buyers are extremely risk averse toward the future.

An investor who is refusing the sale of a company when the majority have given their consent is a toxic business partner. However, the shares they own in the company entitle them to rights that they purchased, and you have to honor that contract as the CEO. These kinds of issues have to be dealt with ahead of time—much earlier than the kickoff of the sale.

On the other hand, we have seen lots of examples where the buyers refuse to sign the documents the day of closing the deal. These are the results of problems much earlier in the process, and left to fester, these problems escalate to deal-breakers. It is imperative to never be blindsided by the necessary approval process internally prior to final signatures from the buy side to avoid these hiccups.

ELEVENTH-HOUR CHANGES MAKE ALL PARTIES FEEL SOUR

No surprises for both sides should be the motto in the last two weeks before signatures. Unfortunately, this is not always the case. We have seen examples from both sides of the table where either the buyers or the sellers request last-minute, material changes. This is a classic blunder that trades short-term gain for long-term issues.

The most egregious version of this is price renegotiation—and this is the easiest way to lose the deal altogether. Founders may point out that their recent growth wasn't appropriately priced-in and the deal took too long to put together; the buyers may highlight issues uncovered in diligence. To each party, they are doing what they believe is fair. It isn't. Perception is reality, and there is no way to avoid coming off as insincere with a material change request.

This is why regular, immediate communication of issues is essential. In general, a problem should not show up in the documents before it is discussed. The very nature of a material change means that the crucial element of alignment is now missing, and losing that in the tail end of the process spells disaster. As the leader, it's your responsibility to bite the bullet: if the issue has not been brought up until the signature process, you will have to live with it. No side should hold the deal hostage over already-negotiated terms.

You must avoid this behavior at all costs or risk giving up the FAIR status of the deal. Even if you get the price increase, is it worth losing trust of the buyer? What if that extra amount comes out of future resources made available inside the parent company? The bill comes due always, and the long-term nature of these engagements will make sure that the problems stashed away today will rear their ugly heads in the near future.

In parallel on the acquirer's side, squeezing the founders on compensation or holdback periods is also a terrible idea at the last minute. A bitter leader will not stick around, no matter the upside, or—far worse than losing talent—they will stick around and be disengaged.

Although there are ways that a deal can die at this phase, you will always be better off in assuming good intent. Push forward as if the deal is going to go through and these will be your partners. That positive attitude will help the integration and growth phase that is so critical post-closing.

CHAPTER 11

HOW SHOULD THE CEO TAKE CARE OF THE TEAM?

B EING AN ENTREPRENEUR IS A DEEPLY EMOTIONAL and fraught experience. It's risky to bet on yourself and take the less-traveled path. This is your dream, your baby, your sacrifice. Often you've risked everything, including important personal relationships, to reach this point. This is your moment of triumph where all the pain and the trips on the emotional roller coaster are finally going to pay off. You've certainly earned the moment to enjoy the spoils of all your labor...but remember, you're not alone, and you didn't do this by yourself.

Now is the time to be magnanimous. Think past yourself, and expand your vision outside of your personal needs. You must remember not only all those whose incredible hard work helped get you to this point but also those who may want to join you on your next adventure—whatever and whenever that might be. As VCs, our eyes and ears perk up when we come across a company where the CEO and their executive team had an exit and then, together as a group, started their next company. That speaks volumes about the team and how they work together.

How you treat your team matters. It's so easy to be selfish, to rationalize how deserving you are, but don't succumb to the greed of the moment. We like to say that true character comes out in the extremes when there is either a lot or very little money to distribute. In our interviews with CEOs and stakeholders, we heard plenty of stories of leaders who fought for their team and took less for themselves—and exactly the opposite, where the CEO maximized their own gains and didn't share with the team or fight for their needs.

The legal documents are important. They are the true north of how distributions are made, and they should be followed to the letter in the spirit of fairness and transparency. If the right thing to do does not match the legal documents, discuss changing the documents in transparency with all parties. If you feel that the distribution isn't fair, then you can always take less and give more to your employees. No one will stop you (especially if you are not taking away from your other shareholders). Don't take refuge in the empty argument of "Well, that's what the documents say." That's not a good enough excuse. If the docs are wrong, morally or otherwise, change them.

When Kevin Systrom sold Instagram to Facebook, Instagram was still a small company. Kevin walked away with over $400 million, while most of his employees received relatively little from the transaction other than having Facebook as their new employer. Only three employees had been there long enough to vest Instagram shares. However, in order for them to convert their shares to Facebook restricted stock units, they needed to pay $300,000. They weren't all that happy. It would have been easy for Kevin to have given each $1 million. He wouldn't have felt it, and it would have been life-changing for each of them.

As a matter of fact, it is common for founders to "make it right" for their teams, even in stressful exits. Collin Wallace, the Founder and CEO of FanGo, did exactly that. After several years, FanGo sold to Grubhub for a modest return to investors. When the company was first founded, Collin made some promises of equity to early employees. But being a first-time founder, he never recorded those equity grants appropriately. Legally, those equity promises did not exist.

When it became time to sell the company, Collin quickly recognized his mistake. He tried to get the board of directors to allocate shares to those employees, but no one was willing to take less. So Collin stepped up and did the honor-able thing: he reduced his proceeds so that he could take care of his employees and honor his word. He never thought twice. It was the right thing to do.

The world of entrepreneurship is small. We believe that in the long run, people want to build companies with CEOs like Collin, not Kevin. And of the two, we know which CEO we'd rather be (or work for).

FINDING BALANCE IN THE WATERFALL BETWEEN INVESTOR RETURNS AND EMPLOYEE RETENTION

There is inherent tension between the investors who have been with you from the early days of your journey and the incentives for the acquiring company. Your investors will want to get paid as much as possible when the transaction closes, while the acquiring company will only care about the future possibilities of the two companies together. For the investors, the value creation ends. For the acquirer, all the value lies in the future.

In order to maximize the value of the acquisition, the vast majority of the time, the acquiring company is going to depend on the existing employees—and the critical knowl-edge they uniquely possess—to stay with the company. The acquirer is therefore incentivized to pay the employees more to stay and give less to the investors because they care about the future and discount the past. Often the CEO is caught in the precarious middle—a difficult terrain to navigate.

According to the National Venture Capital Association (NVCA), over 67 percent of the companies that take in venture capital money pay back less than 100 percent of the capital received at the time of an exit. Think about that: over 67 percent fail. Let's bucket outcomes into three categories:

1. A major win for investors of 5x+ returns
2. A modest win of 1–4x
3. Pennies on the dollar to zero to investors

Major wins are pretty rare and usually mean happy days for all parties. While there might be some grumbling from a shareholder or two about the retention plan for employees (involving both future equity as well as cash incentives), everyone is getting a nice payday, and there are usually pretty few squabbles. Your job as CEO is to be in constant communication with all parties—your shareholders, your employees, and the acquiring company—and make sure that everyone is (mostly) satisfied with the outcome. Being in the middle is never easy, but if you are FAIR, open, and transparent about the logic and reasoning, then it should be pretty straightforward.

Modest wins are a little harder from the investor perspective. There is typically relief after a long and arduous road, and they are glad to come out a little better than whole. Your deal won't return their fund, but it puts some points on the board, and it lets them save face. Most VCs will say thank you, take their money, and be glad to move on to the next one.

Unfortunately, there are some VCs who think the world is a zero-sum game and that they need to maximize their gains from each and every deal. These short-sighted investors will want to squeeze every last penny out of a deal—sometimes to the detriment of their fellow investors and, most certainly, the employees. These VCs don't care about tomorrow; they live in the moment. Hopefully, you don't have investors that look like this, but if you do, this is where you have to be tough and fight for your employees.

You and the acquiring company are still going to depend upon your key employees to stay with the company post-transaction and continue to pour their hearts and souls into their work. They are going to need to be compensated for all their past efforts as well as incentivized to stay.

In the middle of a difficult negotiation, what would happen if the final sale price were a few million less to the shareholders and instead that money went into an employee retention plan? How would your shareholders feel? This is where trust comes in. Your shareholders have to believe in their hearts that you are fighting for their best interests as hard as you are fighting for yours and your employees'. They have to believe in you and your judgment that the best way to maximize the deal and outcome is to find a balance between everyone's needs. This won't be easy. Regular, open, and transparent communication is essential to making everyone feel good about the outcomes.

Human nature can often stray to the dark side. When investors don't know what's going on, they can sometimes assume the worst. Don't let doubt fester. Your job is to always build trust. Once again, trust is the lubricant that can ease tensions and help get deals over the finish line.

A loss for your investors hurts. Everyone is frustrated. No one feels great. An emotional stew of anger, anxiety, and even some relief that this is all finally over mix together and cast a shadow. It's okay to be disappointed. But don't take yourself out of the arena just yet. Stay sharp and purpose driven. How you handle the loss will determine a lot of what happens next.

First, don't be embarrassed. You gave it your all. You have learned many lessons, and you will be smarter and wiser the next time around.

This is where you have to stiffen your spine. Hopefully, you have found a good home for your company and your employees. Your investors are already only getting pennies on their dollars invested. While most will be sanguine, some will be pissed and will look askew at every penny that is going toward employees and not into their pockets. This is a delicate balancing act. There is not a lot of money to go around.

In order to make this transaction work, your key employees will need to stay with the new company and be taken care of.

Do your best. Be sure to get advice from mentors you trust. A great strategy is to share the decision-making on this subject with someone the investor group trusts. It would be awesome if you had an ally on the board. It might be your lead investor or an independent board member who can offload some of the pressure and champion the deal alongside you.

THE GOLDEN RULE OF TRANSPARENCY

CEOs must increase in *transparency* as the deal progresses in *certainty*. A great Scott Wald saying is, "My old pappy used to say undone deals get undone." Or as we say here in Chicago, "It ain't over until the fat lady sings."

As you go along the process, your absence as CEO will be noticed and felt. Key employees will be brought into the due diligence process for either financial or technical reviews, and word will start to leak out.

The most precious commodity you have is the trust between you and your key executives and employees and with your investors and shareholders. You don't want to raise expectations that you ultimately can't deliver upon, nor do you want to spring a major surprise on people. There is an art to finding the balance to both downplay expectations toward the beginning of a process and gradually keep your stakeholders informed as deals increase in their likelihood of closing.

Transparency also leads to building confidence in your judgment and gives you an opportunity to solicit feedback and help during the inevitable bumps in the road. Be prudent and judicious, but don't lose the opportunity to build trust and solicit help in key moments. At the end of the day, use the Golden Rule, and treat people like you would like to be treated. The bottom line is you must trust your team. They got you this far; you can trust them to take you to the finish line.

The best time to negotiate with an employee is before they become one. Negotiating one-off deals with key employees, especially in the midst of an ongoing sale process, is to be avoided at all costs.

As we've discussed, going through the process of selling your company is emotionally fraught and difficult for even the most stoic leaders. Tempers flare, and anxieties take hold—not just for you but also for your key employees.

If they are aware of the sales process (and if they are classified as key employees in the negotiation, then they should be!), they will have a dozen urgent and confusing questions cycling in their minds: *Will I have a decent payout? Am I being treated fairly relative to my peers? Is my job safe? What will I be doing at the acquiring company? Do I even want to stay, regardless of incentives?*

If key employees perceive they are not being dealt with fairly, they can hold up negotiations and even kill deals with intransigence and unrealistic demands. Trust us: it can get really ugly fast.

You'll want to keep these rules in mind:

1. Get your legal paperwork in order. Every single employee should sign an employment agreement that assigns all their intellectual property to the company on their first day on the job. No ifs, ands, or buts. This is crucial. And if you don't have this in place, calmly put this book down and fix it.

2. All employee agreements have to be signed, stored safely, and accounted for in a digital data room. If you are looking for a signed employee agreement during the transaction, it's too late. You are wasting your attorney's time trying to track them down, and it will make you look like an amateur to the acquiring company. Most importantly, it will allow a key employee to have leverage over you because they know the transaction won't close unless they sign. Too many deals have been held up by key employees who wouldn't sign employee agreements without further consideration. The best way to avoid this

situation is to not put yourself into that position in the first place.

3. Assume nothing you do is confidential. If you are forced to cut a special sweetheart deal for a key employee to come along, you can pretty much assume that eventually it will come out, and other employees won't be happy that they did not get the same deal.

4. Create alignment with your executive team and key employees *before* you start the process of trying to sell your company. Sharing this news at the beginning of the process can be precarious, and you'll need to carefully weigh the factors and personalities involved in your particular situation. Because selling your company is all-consuming, you need to keep your team focused on running the company and making sure all necessary balls stay in the air. At the same time, some of your key employees will need to participate in key moments of the due diligence process. Take the time to sit down with each key employee and run through your FAIR criteria. Explain the rationale behind the decision and your vision for success, and be ready to answer some basic questions about what their job and/or outcome might look like.

If they have major issues, this conversation is the time for them to raise them. The earlier key employees are on board with the decision and are comfortable with what it means for them, the more you'll be able to count on them steering the ship ahead, and the harder it will be for them to try to renegotiate at the final hour and hold the deal hostage.

Sometimes you don't have any choice, but if you have run a FAIR and transparent process, built trust with your team, remained generous with their payouts, and painted a future where you continue to be excited to work together, then you shouldn't have to make any special exceptions or renegotiate deals at the eleventh hour.

NEGOTIATING COMPENSATION FOR THE TEAM AND EXECUTIVES: INCENTIVES AND HOLDBACK PERIODS

Nothing is more sensitive than compensation. It's where the rubber meets the road, and if not handled well, it will put the health of the merger on the line. In a startup acquisition, compensation is typically dictated by terms that include holdback periods, where a portion of the proceeds of the company will be distributed based on future results. Holdbacks, like equity vesting, are important tools that the acquiring company uses to incentivize merging employees and align the workforce for a successful integration. Sometimes, performance-based holdback terms can lead to a windfall of higher returns, or conversely, they can be a serious limitation if the merger goes sideways and the expected results aren't delivered.

Today, Jason Seats is the Chief Investment Officer of the global Techstars network. But in 2008, he was in the middle of negotiating the sale of his first startup, SliceHost, to Rackspace. He negotiated performance-based tranches of compensation that would be released based on certain milestones. The first two earn-outs were related to integration, and the last tranche was tied to growth. This last term was hotly debated, but finally both sides agreed to a growth number to hit within a four-year time frame. Jason's team ended up reaching the goal in eighteen months, but the timeline and growth milestones were already set. "We shouldn't have put a cap on the milestone. We should have let it ride for the whole vesting period and kept the meter running. We didn't have faith in ourselves to optimize our compensation."

This certainly is an upside example. Not all deals end this way. The world is full of deals that get written off. If there is a holdback of some of the deal value that is dependent upon future results, then it is critical to make sure that you have in writing all the resources that you will need to execute—and if those resources are not provided, then you still get the holdback. This is also a great moment (if you are the acquiring company) to not make promises you can't keep.

The other things to pay extra special attention to are job titles and pay grades. Most smaller companies don't really pay that much attention to pay grades. Trust us: larger companies do, and this really matters. The difference between a VP, SVP, and EVP can mean hundreds of thousands or even millions of dollars in comp and options. We highlighted this in the term sheet, but it bears repeating here: the difference between a level-five engineer and a level-seven could have a profound impact on someone's career trajectory. Do not wait until after the transaction to research this. It is your responsibility to proactively work with the HR department of the acquiring company and understand how they level and grade each job. Then, on an individual basis, you need to work in partnership with their HR team to make sure each member of your team is appropriately graded and leveled.

This is a core component of the integration plan, and without it, the deal terms will unlikely be FAIR. Ideally, this happens before the final signatures are on the closing documents; the leverage you have for anyone other than the key employees is greatly reduced on the other side of the deal.

EMBRACING "GOLDEN HANDCUFFS" AS TOOLS FOR MUTUAL SUCCESS

It's pretty simple: the acquiring company wants you and all the key employees to stay as long as possible. Most of the time, in addition to the intellectual property, the true asset of any company is the people and the knowledge they have about the product, the market, and the customers. Therefore, most deals are constructed and engineered to place incentives for people to stay longer and penalties if they leave early.

In addition to withholding part of the proceeds of the sale based on future performance benchmarks (as described in the previous section), the acquiring company has three tools at their disposal: how existing options vest, awarding new options in the acquiring company, and creating new bonus structures.

The first thing you have to know is how your current stock option plan is managed. The most critical issue is what happens when a company is sold. Do the options all vest immediately? This is called a single trigger. Or does some portion vest upon the transaction (typically 50 percent) and the remainder vest over a schedule or if the employee is let go post-transaction? This is also known as a double trigger.

Most stock option plans are written with a double trigger. Not surprisingly, this is the one place where the interests of the VC align perfectly with the acquiring company. The VCs know that the people are a very valuable asset to the acquiring company, and they don't want the employees to leave immediately after a sale. Most stock option plans are written with a double trigger to help keep employees from bolting. The current stock option plan is under your control, as approved by your board of directors. You can't rewrite your own plan in the middle of a transaction.

The real negotiating point is what future stock options in the acquiring company are going to be awarded. The amount and the vesting schedule are crucial. Typically, these shares will be granted according to the existing stock option plan of the acquiring company on their standard vesting schedule, which is usually equal to four years. Some companies will try to adjust the vesting schedules of these new shares to be longer than the standard plan. You have to be very thorough and pay close attention. This is one of those "gotchas" that lawyers throw in toward the end of a transaction. Smart CEOs bring this up during the negotiation process and don't wait until the end when all the momentum is to close the deal and all the leverage is with the acquiring company.

NAVIGATING NONCOMPETES AFTER THE TRANSACTION

Lastly, the acquiring company is going to insist that you and your executive team all sign noncompetes. Once again, they will want these to be for as long as possible, and you will want to keep them as short as you can. There are a few considerations to keep in mind, such as:

1. Will you keep on working with the acquiring company post-transaction?

2. How significant a shareholder will you become in the acquiring company? Typically the answer is too small to matter.

3. Do you care? Sometimes the payday is large enough, and you are so burned out, that you have zero desire to go and start something new—especially in that particular field. Sometimes the fires are still burning, and you can't wait for your next company to start. Know thyself. The more you are in touch with how you think about your future, the easier it is to negotiate what you want.

The acquiring company can't keep you on the sidelines indefinitely, and they are going to have to pay up in the form of new consideration to keep you from starting something new. A reasonable noncompete is twelve or eighteen months. Depending upon the deal, it can even go up to two years.

Who knows how you are going to feel in a couple of years after the celebrations are over and your competitive juices start flowing again? While each deal is unique, you should definitely start pushing back if they are asking for a noncompete greater than two years. Don't be afraid to dig deeper and ask questions about what they are trying to protect against. If you feel the opposing deal attorney is being unreasonable, don't settle for them telling you that is what their client wants or this is their "standard" term. If you don't like where this is going, be sure to work in partnership with your deal sponsor to fight on your behalf.

CHAPTER 12

WHAT ARE THE KEYS TO A SUCCESSFUL INTEGRATION?

ONGRATULATIONS! THE DEAL HAS FINALLY closed. The rush of emotions is palpable. Going through the sale of your startup is an emotion amplifier. Happiness becomes intense joy. Frustrations easily spiral into anger and lashing out. Bonds of friendships form even tighter, or you make new lifelong enemies. It's not just the intense last few months of trying to get this deal closed—it's the past decade or more of your life building this company from scratch to get to this moment of triumph.

Not every emotion you feel will be rosy. In the days following SwipeSense's deal closing, and right before the COVID-19 pandemic upended our daily lives, we sat down at a coffee shop. What was meant to be a celebratory conversation quickly turned into an outpouring of emotions from Mert.

His feelings were extreme, and they were all over the place. He felt both elation and gratitude for an awesome moment of success. He felt excitement about the possibilities of the future and hope that he and his team would thrive in their new home. And he felt nervous at the thought of no longer being in control of his own destiny. *Will it all turn out okay?* he wondered.

The conversation we had that day—the wisdom that Mark imparted to Mert and the space that Mert had to vent all his excitement, fears, and frustrations—ultimately laid the foundation for this book.

When we asked for his advice for founders' mental health after exits, Brad Feld had the following to say: "You have to give yourself at least six months to feel your emotions. They will be up, down, and all over the place. They will change daily. Sometimes you won't think about anything. Other days you'll obsess about little things. You'll be disoriented. If it was a graceful parting with a party, you likely have some closure. If it was abrupt without a chance to say goodbye to people, consider a comfortable and proactive way to do that and get closure with the people you want to."

There is no correct way to feel, especially when you randomly hear about the company, encounter a prior teammate, or are told something indirectly that seems challenging, difficult, or just plain wrong. Instead of looking for "correct," just feel and acknowledge your feelings.

If you are depressed or feel depleted, know that is normal. Talk to peers who are founders of other companies and have either sold or departed their business. Allow yourself to be open about how you are feeling with those around you. Don't be ashamed, and know that there is no fast way to "feel better."

Above all, make room for yourself. If you've had a financially successful exit, you now have resources you didn't have before. If you need to earn money to pay for your day-to-day existence, try to find an organization to join that you are excited about. If you are starting a new company, embrace the newness of it.

Most new companies fail. It takes brute force of vision and personality to bend the arc of business success in your favor. It's okay to take a victory lap and bask a little in the glory. Any exit, no matter the final number, means that you have beaten the odds. Believe it or not, now comes the hard part. Time to integrate into your new acquiring company. At this critical juncture, your mindset is everything.

Going into the integration with a bad attitude, having silent resentments from a difficult transaction, and feeling fatigued from a long process is a recipe for disaster. Whatever baggage you have, it's time to jettison. In order to make this transaction work, you will have to be optimistic, let go of past issues, and find a way to bring excitement and hopefulness toward starting a new chapter of your life. Think of this as a new beginning with far greater resources at your disposal and not an end of an emotional roller coaster.

Having met founders who have seen their companies struggle after the exit, we are struck by how surprisingly consistent their message is: how you enter into this new relationship really matters as a predictor of future success.

The world is full of failed transactions, and a surefire way to kill success is for leadership to exit. As you know by now, we are big believers in taking the long view and actively managing key relationships with your reputation.

Now is a great time to stop and be thoughtful about how you want to manage this next chapter in your life. The repercussions of your actions now will leave a much bigger impact on your legacy.

Having sold a startup is one thing. Ensuring that it achieved 10x its potential under the new wing of the acquirer in a reasonable amount of time is an entirely different matter. For starters, it shows that the founder had exactly the right vision. Any new VC evaluating a new investment in the founder will know that there is a good chance that their capital will be taken care of.

Furthermore, a successful integration typically means that your team also landed on their feet. Making your team rich is wonderful, but accomplishing greater heights together is even better. Your greatest asset is the cohesive bond that formed through trials and tribulations, strengthened by things working out in the end.

As a founder, nailing down integration might look like a selfless act—the company has been sold and the responsibility seemingly passed on to the buyer. It couldn't be further from the truth. For your long-term benefit, the smartest thing to do is to make sure the company is successful even without you around.

DEFINING SUCCESS METRICS AND THEIR OWNERSHIP BEFOREHAND WILL SET THE RIGHT EXPECTATIONS

Success will look different to you once the transaction closes. Especially if the sale is FAIR, this means life-changing sums of money for the founding team. This is quite different from the humble beginnings of most technology companies, and it's a wonderful thing. New milestones for you will mean that you are able to aim for greater highs in the future. Just like how success has a new definition for you, there is a new definition for victory for your startup, now part of a larger organization.

As part of defining the rationale, we strongly recommend that you carefully define what success looks like post-merger, including the key metrics that measure it. This exercise should be conducted jointly with your deal sponsor and champion. It's imperative that you have alignment on these expectations for everyone's benefit.

This exercise has two key steps. First, what are the key metrics that define success? Second, and equally as important, what are the key resources necessary to execute toward these metrics? The spirit of these steps is to ensure you can deliver the goods you are held accountable for.

Patrick Sullivan is a hard-charging New Yorker, with a bull-in-a-china-shop personality, and when his last company was acquired by Google, he used that personality to make sure the transaction was a success.

He had been promised a certain head count once he was part of Google. Patrick knew the objectives he signed up for were only possible with a bigger team, but the closing docs didn't spell out his budget (as is customary; otherwise deal docs could get way too complicated).

So when his budget request was turned down, he ended up getting in the face of a Google VP to let him know how he really felt about the situation. (He subsequently got twelve new engineers.)

Patrick says, "You can't take your hands off the wheel. If you are going to be held accountable to certain objectives, so are they." Patrick treated Google like a customer, even after his team was embedded there. They started an internal newsletter so that they were always sharing their metrics and news throughout the company. The team highlighted other divisions, which made people like them and look forward to their updates. It was a constant reminder that they were still there and still a force.

Typical Checklist for a Successful Integration:
Ask for the Playbook from the Acquirer

- ☐ Shared functions versus stand-alone subsidiary
- ☐ HR
- ☐ Finance: key metrics that matter, GAAP accounting, timing, and constraints
- ☐ Brand
- ☐ Sales
- ☐ Back office
- ☐ Budgeting and funding
- ☐ Clear designation of authority

THE RESPONSIBILITY FOR A SUCCESSFUL INTEGRATION FALLS ON EVERYONE'S SHOULDERS

When you are selling to a larger company, it's easy to think that they have all the answers. They have done this many times before. All you have to do is sit back and let the pros take over. We believe strongly that the responsibility for a successful integration is equally shared between both parties. There is much you can do proactively to help ensure a successful post-transaction for all. This is especially important if you have an earn-out, where a portion of the proceeds of the transaction are based on the results post-transaction.

Rishad Tobaccowala, the former Chief Strategy Officer of Publicis, who led the acquisition of many companies under his tenure, gives this piece of advice: "At the start of the new relationship, imagine that it's a year down the road and you are writing your one-year-anniversary press release. Write down all the things that went right and all the things that went wrong. Then, go make a plan on how to ensure the successes and mitigate the mistakes. If there are no sensible ways to avoid the bad things from happening, then don't proceed with the acquisition."

Founders have a special role to play. You are the leader, and setting the tone from the top down has a huge impact. When Alex White sold his company to Pandora, he took extra steps to ensure that once the transition happened, they got out of the "us and them" mentality. When someone on his team asked a question like, "How does Pandora do this?" he always responded, "This is how we do it because we are Pandora."

MAINTAINING FAIR AFTER THE CLOSE IS CRITICAL

If you have followed our mantra through the process, you will be in a fantastic place to kick off the relationship with your acquiring company. However, the world is not static.

Business is constantly evolving. There are good quarters and bad ones. Abundant resources followed by hiring freezes or layoffs. People come and go. Leadership and priorities can shift. Your job is to constantly look at your new business through the FAIR lens:

- **Validate fit:** Are the new people you met in the parent company similar to ones throughout the exit process? Is the culture what you assumed? Are your people happy?

- **Keeping alignment:** As you encounter post-close success and setbacks, do you still have good alignment with key leadership? Is your internal champion still your advocate? Are there any hidden detractors, and how do you win them over?

- **Completing integration:** Is the integration going to plan? Are the resources promised being delivered? If not, what steps do you need to course-correct? What can you do proactively, and where do you need to ask for help?

- **Achieving the rationale:** Most importantly, is the original rationale for the merger still holding up over time? Is your vision greater than how you started the relationship?

Be honest and objective with yourself as you think through and evaluate these questions. It's fine if the answers aren't what you thought they would be—life changes. Your job is to give it your all for as long as you are working toward a FAIR outcome.

Here's a truth about most of us founders. Many of us may have started our own companies to create wealth, but even more importantly, we wanted to be our own boss. We wanted operational freedom. We didn't want anyone else telling us what to do. After the transaction closes, you most certainly have a new boss, along with a new board of directors. As if those were not enough, pair that with a much larger bureaucracy to find your way around. Bonus points if it's a public company and there are outside shareholders that your new CFO is laser-focused on placating. In some ways, this is much more direct and straightforward—no guessing as to whom you need to work with. In other ways, this is a significantly more complicated world to navigate.

It's easy to give up and say, "To heck with it. I've got some cash in my pocket. Adios, amigos!" When those feelings arise, remember that your customers are depending upon you. Your employees who helped get you here and stuck with you through thick and thin are depending upon you. If there are still earn-outs or money held in escrow, your shareholders are depending on you to help fight for its eventual distribution.

This is the part where reputation and relationships matter. It's time to return to the strategy of playing a long game. How you leave a job is every bit as important as how you begin one. You need to do everything you can to solve whatever issues you may be having with the new company. Time to grow up, both as a founder and an executive.

This is easier said than done, so below are a handful of frameworks to work through post-close challenges.

COMMON GROUND IN SHARED VALUES TO RESOLVE CONFLICT

When teaching at Kellogg School of Management at Northwestern University, we like to ask the question, "What is your favorite smell from childhood?" It doesn't matter what country you come from, the color of your skin, the culture you were brought up in, whether you are a conservative or liberal, or if you are in a different department or division than ours—every single person on the planet has a favorite smell from childhood.

It's something that is universal. When you go around a room and ask everyone to share their favorite smell, it always elicits smiles and nods of familiarity. That's the secret. Once you get to know someone, even a little bit, they no longer are the "other." Without thinking of strangers as competition, you are given the freedom to make decisions that are best for everyone. You can think of other people, ask for their help, and navigate the future with everyone's best interests in mind. When you don't do that, when you continue to see your new partners as the "other," bad things will emerge. Us versus them never ends on good terms.

So now that you are on the other side, remove the concept of us versus them. Remember that you are now one unit. Focus on the values that you share; they are like smells from your childhood. These values are the foundation of what made Fit possible; they will still be there once the deal is over the finish line.

Start with the assumption of good intent. If someone is acting in a way that is not helpful or is counterproductive, pause and take a moment to ask yourself why they are acting like they are, and assume they have good intentions—unless proven otherwise.

If you start with the assumption of good intent, what follows naturally is giving them the benefit of the doubt. We all have been in relationships that were highly political, each side measuring their words carefully for the fear of being backstabbed. What about the opposite?

It's incredible to have trust and openness in the core of the relationship, where you feel everyone has each other's back. It's clear which relationship is worth building toward. Reciprocating trust and benefit of the doubt from the start doesn't make you weak; it generates camaraderie and dependability.

If the deal wasn't as successful as you thought it could be, it's easy to begin the new relationship with a head of steam and a chip on your shoulder, thinking you have a lot to prove. If the sale was successful, your new company just paid you a life-changing sum of money to start working together. In either case, now is the time to take a deep breath, be humble, and navigate with grace.

No matter with whom you end up working, open your eyes and pay attention to what made your acquirer really successful. No matter what the company is like, you can learn a lot from them.

Think in a longer time horizon, and invest the most in your reputation and your relationships.

Finally, play the long game. Most founders don't stop with their first venture. You are hopefully going to be around for many more decades to come. How you treat people will always be remembered. Your reputation precedes you and lingers after you for a long time.

There's a Yiddish term that we like: be a "mensch." Treat people with kindness and respect. Honor your promises. Build relationships that go deep; avoid transactional ones. Always have a no-assholes rule. Life is too short to deal with people you don't share values with.

Be the person your children would be proud of.

MOST OF THE JOURNEY IS STILL AHEAD

We hope you have enjoyed reading this book as much as we have enjoyed writing it. It has been such an honor to learn from and with such great business leaders, entrepreneurs, transaction attorneys, and corp dev leaders, and to share our collective stories with you. This book is both a practical guide of best practices and frameworks as well as aspirational, gentle coaching to think in the longer term with encouragement to focus on the legacy of your actions. We'd like to leave you with some final thoughts.

DON'T MAKE SERIOUS FINANCIAL COMMITMENTS
FOR AT LEAST SIX MONTHS AFTER THE CLOSE

Brad Feld wrote eloquently in his book *Startup Life* his advice on what to do when you find yourself staring at your checking account and there is more money in there than you ever imagined.

His simple guidance is to not do anything for at least six months. "People will come out of the woodwork to help you—financial advisors, friends, family, and other successful entrepreneurs who have already been through a big exit of their own. The advice will come fast and furiously, and you will feel the pressure to figure out where to put the money, how to invest it, and whom to hire to help you. Don't succumb to this pressure."[14]

According to Brad, there is no way to filter out who has your best intentions at heart. Some will be there to genuinely help; some will be there for themselves. We agree. Financial advisors can simply see a new client with little experience, or family members might view you as deep pockets that can help bail them out of their financial challenges.

Simply put, by taking a deliberate break from making decisions, you can collect data dispassionately, see what the landscape entails, and let the emotions settle before you start making commitments.

BE HONEST WITH YOURSELF ABOUT YOUR TRACK RECORD

Your track record will depend upon the point of view of who is looking at it. Remember, you have multiple stakeholders:

- Your investors will look at how much they received at the time of closing and how you looked after their interests during the process. Be honest with yourself (assuming you would want to work with them again); how willing will they be to back you in your next company?

- Your employees will see how generous you were at the time of closing; did you go to bat to protect their jobs during the transition and fight for their rights inside the new company? Will they come work for you again? What is the future value of working together with a team you trust?

- How will the corp dev leader and the person who championed the deal to acquire you look at this deal with the perspective of time? Did they stake their reputation on doing your deal? Was it a feather in their cap or something to be ashamed of? Do you think they will want to do business with you again in the future?

There's the story you tell everyone, and then there's the real story of how others feel about you. Do everything in your power to ensure that those stories are one and the same.

IMPROVE THE M&A PROCESS OF YOUR ACQUIRING COMPANY

No transaction is perfect. There are always ways to improve the process. This is actually how this book got started. Mert went through a transaction with several learning moments. Mark coached him to write them down, in the spirit of sharing these learnings with his new company so that (at the appropriate time) when they make their next transaction, it can go smoother for everyone.

We like to map out every process both functionally and—even more importantly—through the lens of an emotional roadmap. You've heard of a product roadmap. Do the exact same thing, but map out the emotions. How does the recipient on the other end *feel* in each step of the process/journey? It's an incredibly useful exercise to go through. How do you want people to feel as they go through an M&A experience with your company?

Remember to be humble. Not everyone is open to feedback. In the spirit of trying to improve their process, because you have fresh eyes (and sometimes raw feelings), you can provide valuable insights in the spirit of making it better for the next transaction.

When you leave, leave well.

We understand that most entrepreneurs aren't built to be in larger companies. Going from being your own boss to chafing against a rigid bureaucracy takes some getting used to. We urge you to be patient. Larger companies have much they can teach you, so hang in there for as long as you can and—importantly—as long as you are contractually committed to do so. Hang in there for your employees and customers who are depending upon you.

But sometimes you just have to go. And when you leave, leave well. Be open. Be transparent. Give plenty of notice. For goodness's sake, whatever you do, try your hardest never to burn bridges. Maintain the integrity of relationships you care about, and ensure your reputation is solid and that you can hold your head high.

RELATIONSHIPS MATTER WAY MORE THAN YOU THINK

Who knows what your future will hold? With a successful track record, some money in the bank, and some real operating knowledge and wisdom, where will that take you? Whatever path you end up pursuing, you can bet that some of the people you have interacted with in this company will intersect with you again down the road.

As VCs, we love to see exec teams who worked together previously, had a successful exit, and, through that pressure cooker, bonded to the extent that they want to continue on together as a team. It really says a lot about the quality of trust between them and the mutual confidence in each other's abilities.

Investors love to invest in people they already know and trust. Corp dev leaders like to invest in people they trust. Strategic channel partners like to partner with companies led by people they trust. See a pattern here? Relationships really matter. They are some of your principal assets. Manage these assets like anything else that is precious to you. You will be shocked how often you will run into people from today somewhere in your future.

PAY IT FORWARD, AND BE GENEROUS OF TIME AND SPIRIT

You just had an exit—hopefully, a life-changing event for you and your family. You took huge risks and worked your ass off. Your actions put you in the position to finally cash out. The truth is, as we talked to dozens of CEOs—and as we have experienced ourselves—there is also an element of luck and timing involved. Karma just smiled down upon you. Now is the time to smile back.

Our collective job is to pay it forward and leave this world better off than we found it. Be a mentor to a struggling entrepreneur. You will have so much wisdom, insight, and real-world experience to share. Open up your network to help others. To the extent you can, invest back into deserving entrepreneurs. You are now part of the flywheel of success that begets success.

STAY HUMBLE AND GROUNDED

After having sold your company, you are flooded with many intense and competing emotions, and if it was a successful exit, then you are probably feeling pretty good about yourself. You want to climb the highest hill and shout out to the world at the top of your lungs, "Fuck you, world, I did it!" You should absolutely do that...in the shower, to yourself. Go ahead and indulge yourself and let it rip. It will feel great.

Out there in the real world, you will be asked often to tell your story. It will be so tempting to start off with the words, "Well, I..." Stop yourself. Practice the following: "It was a team effort. I have so many people to thank who made this possible."

Additionally, we urge you to think carefully about courting or encouraging publicity. It's no one's business how much money you made, and there can be unintended consequences from broadcasting that information widely. When Mark sold Kinesoft to SoftBank in 1995, his neighbor was a journalist for the *Chicago Tribune* and asked to interview him about it. Next thing you know, the article was on the front page of the business section. His wife and family were caught off guard by the family's business that was now being talked about among relatives and classmates in their suburban Chicago community. This was an unintended consequence that, in retrospect, he wished he had avoided.

Remember that credit travels down in an organization, while responsibility travels up. Resist the temptation to talk about yourself and what you accomplished. Talk about all the people who came together to make this possible and a success. In the event of failure, take ownership and move on.

Your success is a given. Your role is understood and assumed. You will actually build a much better reputation by being humble. This might come as a slight shock to you, but you are now a superhero to the next generation of entrepreneurs who will want to be and act just like you. Show them your better self. We know you can do it and can't wait to hear the story of the right exit for you and the FAIR deal you made.

ACKNOWLEDGMENTS

FOR MARK ACHLER

Writing this book has been a profoundly humbling experience, as all acts of creation are. When I began this journey, I wanted to share everything I had learned about navigating the exit process after decades in this business with the next generation of entrepreneurs. What I did not anticipate was how much I would learn from all of the amazing founders, corporate development professionals, bankers, and lawyers who so graciously gave their time, support, and encouragement to this effort. Having the support of all of these outstanding leaders and operators, who also thought this book was important and needed to be written, has been a highlight of my career. So I have a lot of people to thank.

This book needed to be written, and it would not have been possible without my daughter Emily Achler. Emily is an outstanding writer and editor, and she is an entrepreneur herself. She has been part of the *Exit Right* book from the very beginning as a project manager, research assistant, writer, and editor. Her insights as a reader and early-stage entrepreneur were critical in shaping the material, and her project management skills kept the book moving forward. Speaking as a father, there is no greater joy than working collaboratively with your daughter and being able to witness (and beam with pride at) everything she is capable of.

I am truly blessed in life with a wonderful family; my wife of nearly forty years, Marcie, and my two other daughters, Sarah and Haley. Our family is and has always been the main source of inspiration and motivation in my life.

A deep and profound thank you to the entire MATH Venture Partners team for your patience and support. You contributed to interviews, shared your stories, helped connect us to folks in your network, and supported Mert and me in the long process of researching and writing. Troy Henikoff, Dana Wright, Kristie Domzalski, Neal Sáles-Griffin, Elisa Sepulveda, and my old friend David Semmel. Thank you. I'm proud every day to have you as my colleagues.

We interviewed dozens of experts who contributed to

the writing of this book. Some of the people we interviewed were old friends whose advice and counsel I often seek: Samir Sirazi, Scott Wald, Gregg Kaplan, Herb Fockler, and Troy Henikoff. You are mensches. Thank you for your friendship and advice. Rishad Tobaccowala is one of the smartest people I know. Period. He is an amazing writer and synthesizer of complex topics. He was one of my first stops when we began writing, and his advice and support have been invaluable.

The founders and operators who spoke with us about their lessons learned are the heroes of this book: Alex White, Rebecca Sholiton, Jennifer Saxton, Andee Harris, Jay Hoffman, Anne Bonaparte, Patrick Sullivan, Mike Shannon, Andrew Gadzecki, and Collin Wallace. You are amazing leaders who exemplify the courage it takes to get into the arena. In contributing to this book, you also exemplify the "give first" mentality that has personally guided me throughout my career and that I hope to instill in future leaders.

The Techstars network, including Brad Feld, Amos Schwartzfarb, and Jason Seats, has supported this book in numerous ways. With people like you at the helm, the Techstars network continues to get bigger and better. We hope this book continues to add value and complements your tremendous work in *Venture Deals* and *Levers*.

Brad Nevin shone a light on the perspective of a board member going through a transaction. Stan Christensen gave us a look at how investment bankers see the world. And Rob

Marcus, former CEO of Time Warner Cable, generously took several meetings with us to share stories of battles lost and won.

Cliff Shaw and Don Loeb both contributed a ton of expertise to the book. Their insights formed the foundation of several chapters. Both were indispensable to this effort.

To Larry Chu, Co-Chair of Global Tech M&A at Goodwin, we owe a debt of gratitude. The legal questions and ramifications that are a part of the exit process are so crucial and yet so unfamiliar for most. Thank you for your help decoding the mystery in the service of helping more entrepreneurs successfully navigate these choppy waters.

One of the main lessons of this book is the importance of empathy and relationship building in business transactions. We want founders to understand the corporate development mindset within the acquiring company, and we want corporate development professionals to similarly understand where founders are coming from. We set out to lift up the curtain on the previously hidden world of corporate development, and we are just thrilled with the results. A huge thank you to our new friends at Pinterest, Twitch, Snowflake, Atlassian, Facebook, PayPal, and Google who helped us paint the full M&A picture: Gary Johnson, Hilary Shirazi, Sarah Hughes, Chris Hecht, Dave Sobota, Peter Sanborn, Maneet Singh, Austin Johnson, and Stefan Williams.

As first-time authors, we entered into a world of the unknown. Thank you to Scribe Media, JeVon McCormick,

Maggie Rains, Kacy Wren, and all of the editors and proof-readers at Scribe. We thank you. Entrepreneurs everywhere thank you.

I want to say a few things about my partner on *Exit Right*, Mert Hilmi Iseri. I first met Mert when he was a brand-new entrepreneur just out of college, ready to take on the world. Today, Mert is more battle-tested, but his zeal for life, for pushing the boundaries and creating new possibilities, is still burning bright. Founders dream of what's possible, and then they go out and do it. They have these "crazy" ideas—like, say, writing a book(!) that they just don't drop. As Mert would say, our collaboration and partnership has been one of "game recognizing game." It's been an honor and a privilege, sir. I can't wait to see what comes next.

And finally, I want to call out my father, Howard Achler, who is no longer with us in person but is always with me in spirit. He was a brilliant engineer, tinkerer, and computer buff who instilled in me a passion for technology, eternal curiosity, and boundless optimism for the future.

FOR MERT ISERI

This is the first book of a series on lessons learned in my practice as a founder.

Entrepreneurship is a craft. It's a scientific endeavor, challenged by limited datasets of personal experiences and costly mistakes. The ones that make the distance in this journey are the ones who treat their process of "trial and error" with an eye toward long-term mastery. I have dedicated my life to this humbling journey. The publishing of *Exit Right* signifies a moment of transition, leaving SwipeSense to start my next chapter.

This book is my first attempt to share what I wish I'd had as an entrepreneur with other founders. It has been written with the generosity of many others who left their mark on me.

Firstly, I want to acknowledge my co-founders, Yuri Malina and Jori Hardman, who, through thick and thin, shared this adventure with me. They kept pushing me and each other to be better, and I'm eternally grateful for their partnership. In my heart, I know that we will be climbing many mountains together in the future.

Second, I'm grateful for all of the founders, bankers, lawyers, and M&A executives who have generously shared their wisdom with us in making this book happen. After going through my own exit, I knew there were huge gaps in my perspective. Dozens of experts shared their hard-earned lessons with us. Their advice will live on to hopefully help thousands of founders who are facing the difficult task of selling their companies. I want to call out Brad Feld for generously agreeing to write a foreword and Larry Chu for his priceless advice during the writing process.

Third, I want to thank Emily Achler, our editor, project manager, and thought partner who brought this book to life. Writing a book is a stressful experience, and you made it enjoyable for all of us.

Finally, I want to call out my mentor, co-author, and dear friend Mark Achler. You have given me a North Star to strive toward with my life. You've shown me that ambition can coexist with kindness and that when the dust settles, there is nothing more important than family. I hope this book made you proud, and I'm looking forward to writing many more together.

DISCLAIMER

Any opinions expressed in this book are those of the respective authors and not of UBS or any of its subsidiaries and/or affiliates, and may differ or be contrary to opinions expressed by other business areas or groups of UBS as a result of using different assumptions and criteria. The reader should not construe the contents of this book as any legal, tax, accounting, regulatory or other specialist or technical advice, or services or investment advice, or a personal recommendation from UBS. UBS makes no representation or warranty, either express or implied, in relation to the accuracy, completeness or reliability of the information contained herein. Neither UBS nor any of its affiliates, or their respective directors, officers, employees or agents accept any liability for any loss or damage arising out of the use of all or any part of this book or reliance upon the information contained herein.

UBS Financial Services Inc., its affiliates and its employees do not provide tax or legal advice. You should consult with your personal tax and/or legal advisor regarding your personal situation.

Important information about brokerage and advisory services. As a firm providing wealth management services to clients, UBS Financial Services Inc. offers investment advisory services in its capacity as an SEC-registered investment adviser and brokerage services in its capacity as an SEC-registered broker-dealer. Investment advisory services and brokerage services are separate and distinct, differ in material ways and are governed by different laws and separate arrangements. It is important that you understand the ways in which we conduct business and that you carefully read the agreements and disclosures that we provide about the products or services we offer. For more information, please review client relationship summary provided at ubs.com/relationshipsummary.

MATH Venture Partners Management, LLC, Presented By, LLC, Scribe, LLC and the authors are not affiliated with UBS Financial Services Inc.

The key symbol and UBS are among the registered and unregistered trademarks of UBS. UBS Financial Services Inc. is a subsidiary of UBS AG. Member FINRA/SIPC. IS2106243

ENDNOTES

1   Any opinions expressed in this book are those of the respective authors and not of UBS or any of its subsidiaries and/or affiliates. UBS makes no representation or warranty, either express or implied, in relation to the accuracy, completeness, or reliability of the information contained in this book. See additional disclaimers at the back of the book.

2   UBS Investor Watch 1Q18, "Who's the boss?" February 2018.

3   UBS Global Wealth Management invested assets exceed $3.2 trillion as of June 30, 2021; statements of the market position for Global Wealth Management are UBS's estimates based on published invested assets and internal estimates.

4   UBS Financial Services Inc., its affiliates, and its employees do not provide tax or legal advice. You should consult with your personal tax and/or legal advisor regarding your personal situation.

5   Zappos.com, "Jewelry | Zappos True Customer Story," YouTube video, November 5, 2017, https://www.youtube.com/watch?v=pfC4NFzbQ2k.

6　"Sony-Columbia Pictures: Lessons from a Cross Border Acquisition," *IBS Center for Management Research*, accessed August 9, 2021, https://www.icmrindia.org/casestudies/catalogue/Business strategy2/Sony-Columbia Pictures Cross Border Acquisition.htm.

7　"Hart-Scott-Rodino Act Thresholds Decrease for 2021," *Cooley*, February 1, 2021, https://www.cooley.com/news/insight/2021/2021-02-01-hart-scott-rodino-act-thresholds-decrease-2021.

8　Sarah Friar, *No Filter: The Inside Story of Instagram* (New York: Simon & Schuster, 2020).

9　We want to give special thanks to the Co-Chair of the Global Tech M&A Practice at Goodwin Procter Law, Larry Chu. As a partner with over $150 billion in transactions under his belt, he generously provided his wisdom in the making of this chapter. He is also an active investor, and we highly recommend working with someone extraordinary like him on your startup.

10　Brad Feld and Jason Mendelson, *Venture Deals: Be Smarter than Your Lawyer and Venture Capitalist*, 3rd ed. (Hoboken, NJ: Wiley, 2016).

11　Chris Hecht, "The Atlassian Term Sheet," *Atlassian*, December 16, 2019, https://editorial.atlassian.net/wiki/spaces/ED/pages/262284/The+Atlassian+Term+Sheet.

12　Annie Duke, *Thinking in Bets: Making Smarter Decisions When You Don't Have All the Facts* (New York: Portfolio/Penguin, 2018).

13　James P. Carse, *Finite and Infinite Games: A Vision of Life as Play and Possibility* (New York: Free Press, 1986).

14　Brad Feld and Amy Batchelor, *Startup Life: Surviving and Thriving in a Relationship with an Entrepreneur* (Hoboken, NJ: Wiley, 2013).